What students are saying:

"I had an amazing experience with this company in terms of both the quality of the products I received as well as my interaction with their experts. I had applied to medical schools without success in the past, had got rejected after interview multiple times, so I signed up for their platinum interview package. The experts were super knowledgeable, patient and caring. They helped me develop confidence and took their time to go over every scenario we practiced; the feedback they provided me was extremely helpful and played a big role in helping me gain admission to several schools, including my top choice, this year. I can only say superlative things about BeMo Academic Consulting and I highly recommend this company for application and interview preparation for professional schools." – ARS

"Choosing BeMo Academic is one of the best decisions I've made. It offers variety of services beginning with application reviews and ending with interview preps. I took the course for dental school interview prep, and it made me realize how unfamiliar I was with the style of those interviews. I would like to note that BeMo not only prepared me for professional interviews, but also taught me skills to treasure for a lifetime. With BeMo you will learn appropriate interview behavior, choice of vocabulary, body language and most importantly - the right mindset. Highly recommending signing up to improve your skills and confidence as a future leader!" – Gaya

"What an outstanding interaction! I have had a fantastic experience working with BeMo! From start to finish I would say that the experience has improved more than my chances of success but also how I am communicating at work! It has been a great experience and I highly recommend it even if you just want to develop how you interact with people and how you manage information and communication in your work life! I most recently worked with Dr Ashley Grimaldi who gave me exceptional feedback that I hope to put into action in just two days! Throughout the experience I haven't just prepared for the interview, I have changed how I perceive my chances of success and it has been very enlightening! I highly recommend BeMo." – Mike

"Was really happy with the panel mock interview. Wasn't expecting the BeMo expert to be a doctor on the other end and an admissions expert. He gave excellent feedback, directions and answered all my questions. I would strongly recommend this service to anyone who wants to get into medical school. It puts you to the test as if it's the real thing. Worth every dime. Make sure to take your first mock interview a several weeks before the actual interview." – Arno

"I did a mock panel interview with Sam. He simulated a real interview extremely well, but the real value of the session was in the tailored feedback he provided. My continued preparation for my medical school interview next month is largely guided by the feedback I received. I would highly recommend doing at least a couple mock interviews with BeMo." – Brad

"BeMo experts provided me with individualized feedback and constructive criticism of my weaknesses. I developed the proper mindset for both CASPer and interviews and I can tangibly feel the improvement. I plan to continue working with BeMo services to further improve my skills during the upcoming medical school application cycle." – Sahar

"I just recently left an interview with one of my PA programs and I can sincerely say I believe I did fantastic. And I have Adam and Peter to thank for that. Adam gave me practical tools to organize my thoughts without sounding rehearsed. That was so very important to me because I wanted my personality as well as my academic ability to shine through and I believe It did. Peter, the night before my interview really helped me take a deep breath and remember that I was capable of amazing things! He helped me tap back into my confidence that was being overshadowed by my nerves. Thank, thank you! After having many different mock interviews over the last several days I think it's really important that interviewers take the time to help their client put together their thoughts in terms of their own life story and their experiences and NOT just give them examples of how to organize their thoughts. Students sometimes

struggle putting what makes them a good candidate into words- I believe it is an interviewers' job to help them do that." – Osa

"My experience with BeMo was excellent. I am a third-year applicant and had three Canadian medical school interviews – I recently accepted my offer to attend University of Toronto's medical school! I decided to prepare for interviews with BeMo, and was assigned two coaches, Karim and Lauren, who were professional, kind, and provided excellent feedback - which is the most important part of interview preparation in my opinion. As past admission committee members, they expertly spotted areas I was weak in, and patiently worked with me to strengthen these areas. The standard of interview preparation with BeMo is extremely high, and I would not hesitate to recommend their services for any stage of the application process." – Matthew

"Matthew has been extremely helpful. He is an exceptional coach with practical methods for breaking down and solving the most complicated of medical school interview problems. He pointed out my interview strengths and areas of improvement. Thank you for the incredibly helpful session today morning." – Amber S.

"I used BeMo both for my application and interview prep. I am from Ontario and applied to 11 Canadian medical schools. BeMo helped me prep my applications and present myself so that I managed to get 4 interviews. The interview prep was amazing - they taught me how to understand and break down a question so that I could present my own ideas well, and they helped me come up with ways to best describe my own personal experiences." – Jesse

"I had second interview practice session before my interview and again the quality of consultant never failed to prove itself. The second consultant provided ways to structure my responses which I believed made my answer succinct, to the point and organized. Moreover, he offered some advice based on the school offering the interview which help me to make appropriate changes before the real interview. Both sessions definitely took out the nerves before the interview and I was composed, clear and coherent when facing the interviewer in the real deal." – WW

"My experience with Dr. Ibukunoluwa was the perfect amount of practice, feedback and positive encouragement needed for my last second interview as an Internal Medicine candidate. In the span of ~1.5 hours, we went through a thorough mock interview, reviewed my answers and he went above and beyond in answering some of my more candid questions towards his thoughts/opinions. Before I signed up at BeMo Academic Consulting, I fully admit of balking due

to the price but fully endorse the level of professionalism and honesty provided by Dr. Ibukunoluwa in helping me polish my interviewing capabilities." – Roland

"This was my third mock interview with BeMo and Dr. Cao. All practices have been extremely useful. The company has great consultant that are knowledge and passionate. This make a big difference. Highly recommend." – Ravneet

"Just wanted to drop you a line and let you know that I was accepted into all three schools (Queen's, Mac and U of T) but will be accepting U of T. Thanks again for all the help in the process [application review, CASPer prep & interview prep] and I look forward to seeing you around campus / hospitals in the near future." – Sameer

"Great experience and great opportunity to get a sense of what the real interview will be like! Thanks so much Connor for your excellent feedback and help!" – Customer

"My interviewer helped me not only with feedback after my traditional panel mock interview, but she also spent some time helping me with responses for additional interview questions from previous interviews I've had that I thought were hard." – Anthony

"Had several interview practice sessions with Matthew. He was excellent and provided constructive feedback and took time to go through scenarios, structures and answer questions in depth. Thanks for your help!" – Dani

"Braydon was my interviewer. He was awesome and really helpful. I have experience in a healthcare field and a master's program, and he was able to help me utilize all my experiences in the best way possible. Structuring my answers was something I needed help with, and Braydon taught me a really simple way to approach it. This was awesome!" – Raza A.

"Great experience and great opportunity to get a sense of what the real interview will be like! Thanks so much Connor for your excellent feedback and help!" – Customer

"I learned so much from Samuel! Being older than most applicants and not having friends currently on the same journey I had no idea where to start or how to even organize my answers. Samuel was very helpful and let me know where I need to focus in order to have a successful interview." – Customer

"I just finished my second mock interview with Braydon. He always took time to give me thorough feedback on each interview question - He highlighted specific areas that I did well and aspects that I could work on. I truly appreciate his willingness to share how he would answer my questions if he was the interviewee. Real examples always help me learn better! Thanks Braydon."
– Customer

"Excellent interview prep program. All interviewers are top quality with respect to their expert feedback." – Customer

BeMo's Ultimate Guide to Medical School Interview

How to Ace Your Med School Interview without Memorizing any Sample Questions

BeMo® Academic Consulting Inc.

ISBN: B087SJRB8K

ISBN 13: 9798642050163

Important Notice. Please read carefully. By using this book, you acknowledge that you have read, understood, and agreed with our terms and conditions below.

Disclaimer: Please note that certain parts of this book are similar or identical to the content presented in BeMo's interview video training course and BeMo's Ultimate Guide to Multiple Mini Interview (MMI). If you have purchased BeMo's video course or one of our Multiple Mini Interview (MMI) preparation programs, you will have access to most of the content presented, although certain parts of this book are completely new material and are not included in our video course or MMI preparation programs. Furthermore, if you have purchased any of our CASPer prep video training, programs, or book, you will notice some similarities. This is because CASPer and MMI were created by the same university and are thus very similar. Nevertheless, there are many differences which we have highlighted in this book. Moreover, doing well on CASPer does not necessarily translate to doing well on MMI and vice versa. You may choose to use this book as a starting point in your preparation or as a complement to our MMI programs at your discretion.

We have conducted thorough research to provide accurate information to help you prepare for and ace your medical school interview. However, readers are responsible for their own results and must always adhere to official interview instructions.

BeMo is not affiliated with, nor does it endorse, any of the organizations mentioned, including, but not limited to universities, colleges, official test administrators, or any external websites, unless explicitly indicated otherwise.

Score increase claims refer to score increases observed in practice simulations.

CONTRIBUTING AUTHORS

Dr. Behrouz Moemeni, Ph.D., founder & CEO @ BeMo

Ms. Ronza Nissan, M.A., admissions expert & lead trainer

Dr. Veena Netrakanti, M.D., admissions expert & associate lead trainer

Dr. Adam Studniarek, M.D., admissions expert

Dr. Meng Yang, Ph.D., admissions expert

Contents

Acknowledgments

We would like to thank our students and their parents for putting their trust in us and giving us the privilege of being a part of their journey. You have inspired us and taught us lessons we would not have learned on our own. Thank you for your continued support and for investing in our mission. You are the reason we get up in the morning.

We would like to thank the countless number of admissions deans, directors, officers, pre-health advisors and school counselors who have 'unofficially' supported our mission. Thank you for encouraging us and, most importantly, thank you for making us think critically. We appreciate what you do, and we understand the impossible task you face each and every single day.

A huge thanks to our team members, both past and present. BeMo wouldn't be what it is today without you.

And, of course, a huge thanks to our family and friends who have been unconditionally supportive, even when we couldn't spend as much time with them because of our obsession with our mission here at BeMo.

Foreword

First, CONGRATULATIONS for making the commitment to educate yourself to become a competitive applicant, a better person, and a better future professional. The fact that you have purchased this book tells us that you understand the value of continuous learning and self-improvement. The world rewards individuals who continuously seek to educate themselves because *knowledge is power*. Before we dive in, let's get on the same page about the purpose of this book, who this book is for, who it is NOT for, and why you should listen to us. But first, a few words from our founder and CEO, Behrouz Moemeni.

Why I Founded BeMo®: Message from BeMo's Founder and CEO, Dr. Behrouz Moemeni

Sometimes you must do what's necessary, even if the chances of success are slim to none. Students often ask me what gets me up in the morning and what motivated me to found BeMo. The answer for me is rather simple and has remained the same since day one.

I started BeMo with my cofounder, Dr. Mo Bayegan, in 2013 – see why it's called "BeMo" now? Our partnership began when we first met back in high school in 1996, and then later solidified during our undergraduate and graduate years.

We both felt every student deserves access to higher education, whatever his or her social status or cultural background, because education is the best way to introduce positive change in our world.

Sadly, I believe most of the current admissions practices, tools and procedures are biased, out-dated, and more importantly, scientifically unproven. Therefore, in 2013, as Mo and I were finishing our graduate studies, we decided to create BeMo to make sure no one is treated unfairly due to flawed admissions practices.

At the time, I was finishing my Ph.D. studies in Immunology at the University of Toronto, which was a transformational educational experience. I had the privilege of working with one of the sharpest minds in the field, Dr. Michael Julius. He taught me many things over the years, but two lessons stayed with me: 1) There is tremendous value in having curiosity about scientific or technological innovations to seek the truth rather than confirm one's own opinions, and 2) what you do has to be the reason that gets you up in the morning. Though I wasn't his best student, I was still relatively successful. I won 19 awards, I was invited to 7 international conferences, and I even had an unsolicited job offer before I had defended my thesis. The job would give me a secure source of income and I would have been able to start paying my mounting student debt, but I ultimately decided to abandon a career in academia. Instead, I chose to start BeMo. Despite having many well-established competitors and an overall slim chance of success, I felt – and I still do to this day – that the mission was well worth the risk. I truly believe what we do here at BeMo adds more value to each of our students' lives than anything else I could have done in academia, and I would not trade it for the world.

Over the years, our amazing and steadily growing team has helped many students navigate the admissions process. We really couldn't have done it without them, and it's been a privilege to teach with them and learn from them over the years. (Thanks for sticking with us!)

We are aware that our methods are controversial in some circles; innovative ideas often are. However, we are confident in our belief – and the scientific literature supports this – that current admissions practices are rife with bias and must be improved.

This is why, in 2017, I founded another independent company called SortSmart®, which has created what I consider to be the fairest, most scientifically sound, and cost-effective admissions screening tool out there. I invite you to visit SortSmart.io to learn more and tell your university admissions office to bring SortSmart to your school.

In the meantime, while SortSmart is gathering momentum, we, at BeMo, will continue to support students just like you to make sure no group of students is treated unfairly. You can rest assured that we will not stop until our goals have been achieved.

To your success,

Behrouz Moemeni, Ph.D.

CEO @ BeMo

A bit about us: BeMo Academic Consulting (BeMo)

We are an energetic academic consulting firm, comprised of a team of researchers and professionals who use a proven, evidence-based, and scientific approach to help prospective students with career path development and admissions to undergraduate, graduate, and professional programs such as medicine, law, dentistry, and pharmacy.

We believe your education is one of your most valuable assets and learning how to become a great future professional or scholar doesn't need to be complicated. We also believe that each student deserves access to higher education, regardless of his or her social status or cultural background. However, most of the current admissions practices, tools, and procedures are biased, outdated, and more importantly, scientifically unproven.

Our goal is to create truly useful (and scientifically sound) programs and tools that work and provide more than just some trivial information like the other admissions consulting companies out there. We want to make sure everyone has a fair chance of admission to highly competitive professional programs despite current biases in admissions practices.

We do whatever it takes to come up with creative solutions and then test them like mad scientists. We are passionate about mentoring our students, we're obsessed with delivering useful educational programs, and we go where others dare not to explore.

Why should you listen to us?

We are the leaders in admission preparation for extremely competitive professional schools. Each year, we help thousands of students gain admission to top schools around the world by assisting them with their application documents and preparing them for CASPer and interviews of all styles, including Multiple Mini Interviews (MMIs), traditional interviews, and video interviews. We have an exceptional team of practicing professionals, medical doctors, scholars, and scientists who have served as former interview evaluators and admissions committee members. Learn more about our experts at BeMoAcademicConsulting.com.

What we are about to share with you in this book is based on what we learned in our sought-after paid training programs. What we offer works and it works consistently. In fact, research has shown that our programs can increase applicants' application scores by up to 27% in simulated interviews. Our programs are in high demand and we are certain they will also work for you.

Why did we write this book?

There is so much misinformation surrounding the admissions process, from online forums to university clubs, and even some university guidance counselors and official test administrators. While some of this information is well-intended, the level of inaccuracy is astounding. In particular, the credibility of online forums can be called into question because it is not clear who the authors are or what motivations they have. These forums are frequently filled with fake profiles, some of them official university administrators and test administrators trying to control the flow of information so only their version of 'facts' is distributed. To make matters worse, some of these forums offer sponsorship opportunities to companies, which puts them in a financial conflict of interest. Also be wary of information from most student clubs because, again, these organizations frequently form financial relationships with companies to garner support for their operations and, as a result, receive and distribute one-sided information. Additionally, most books available are incomplete and tend to have a narrow focus on teaching you interview 'tricks', without offering any meaningful strategy on how to ace any possible *type* of interview question. They do not focus on the big picture that is essential to your success, both as an applicant and as a future practicing professional.

What is this book about?

This book is about helping you develop the fundamental tools so you can become a mature, ethical, and knowledgeable individual, which is essential to your future profession. While we spend a considerable amount of time walking you through how to prepare for your medical interview, it is important to always remain focused on the big picture.

Who is this book for and who is it NOT for?

If the medical program you are applying to requires you to participate in an interview, then this book is perfect for you. Regardless of where you are in your preparatory process, this book has something for you, provided that you are willing to put in the hard work and invest in yourself. Getting into a competitive professional school is challenging, as is becoming a practicing professional. The journey is also very consuming of your time, money, and energy.

We do *not* share any quick 'tricks', 'shortcuts', or 'insider scoops' like some of the other books you may find because:

a) You cannot trick your way to becoming a mature, ethical professional. Rather, you must put in long hours of self-training. If a professional athlete must train for years – on average ten years, hence the 'ten-year rule' – to get to that level of proficiency, wouldn't it make sense that our future doctors, lawyers, dentists, and pharmacists, who deal with people's lives, would need to put in the effort to learn the necessary skills?

b) Sharing 'tricks' or 'insider scoops' would be highly unethical. You should be immediately alarmed if a book or admissions company claims to be sharing 'insider' information.

c) We have a strict policy at BeMo to only help students who are genuinely interested in becoming a caring future professional who want to serve their communities, not those who may be primarily motivated by financial security, status, or social pressure from their parents and peers, and certainly not those who are looking for an easy, cheap shortcut to get in.

How should you read this book?

We recommend that you first read the book cover to cover and then come back to specific chapters for a detailed read. The more you read the book, the more you will internalize the essential strategies. It is important to note that there is a lot of information in this book, and if you try to do everything at once, it may be overwhelming and lead to discouragement. Therefore, it is best that you first read this book for pleasure from cover to cover, then gradually start to implement our recommendations.

To your success,
Your friends at BeMo

CHAPTER I

What is a Medical School Interview?

The medical school interview is often the last and most dreaded step prior to receiving the highly anticipated acceptance letter. Invested students know how much work it takes to get to that point. They sacrifice weekends and social time to maintain their academic performance and attend preparatory programs to boost their standardized test scores. Countless hours are poured into volunteering, research, and shadowing physicians. Yet, this is not enough. As you know, medical programs receive enormous amounts of applications each year, and must therefore opt to interview promising candidates to further select the best students for the limited number of seats they offer.

This is where we come in to help. Whether you are waiting to receive interview invitations or preparing for an upcoming interview, this book will give you the essential tools you need to clear this final hurtle. We will walk you through the various interview types used by medical programs and how to approach each one. However, before we do that, we need to first look at the history of medical school interviews to understand why they are used and how they have evolved.

History and Rationale Behind the Use of Medical School Interviews

The first medical school, Schola Medica Salernitana, was founded in the 9th century in southern Italy. Their admissions criteria were based entirely on the financial status of the applicants – those who could afford eight years of medical training – rather than previous academic success, critical reasoning, or interpersonal skills. Although finances determined admissions, Schola Medica Salernitana published several guides on how to treat patients respectfully – including guides for patient care and bedside manner. This indicates that, since the inception of medical training, the healthcare profession has always valued patient care, regardless of admissions criteria.

Hundreds of years later, in 1765, the University of Pennsylvania established the Perelman School of Medicine, the first medical school in North America. The Perelman School of Medicine, and other institutions that opened around that time, maintained the basic principles established by Schola Medica Salernitana – the importance of serving others and equal emphasis on both technical and interpersonal skills. However, wanting to train students who already had the foundations necessary the complete their studies, early North American medical schools based their admission criteria on previous academic success, leaving students' interpersonal skills to be developed during medical school training.

In the 1920s, standardized testing was first included in the admissions process. The original test, created by F.A. Moss and colleagues, was initially called the "Moss Test" and thought to be a measure of readiness for medical school. It was later revamped and renamed as the Medical College Admissions Test, commonly known as the MCAT. However, accepting students based on standardized testing and academic history resulted in attrition rates as high as 50%

amongst medical students. As if to make matters worse, medical schools responded by increasing academic requirements.

In the late 1990s and early 2000s, professional regulatory bodies of medicine began conducting studies to understand the major complaints that the public had about their health care providers. One study published in the *New England Journal of Medicine* revealed that the number one complaint most patients had about their physicians had nothing to do with their clinical skills and competencies, but rather with the doctors' emotional intelligence and soft skills (N Engl J Med 2005; 353:2673-2682). For example, patients complained that their doctors were not compassionate or empathetic enough, or simply did not have good communications skills. Based on this evidence, professional faculties were asked to devise admissions procedures that selected candidates who not only had a great academic record, but also possessed strong soft skills.

Thus, medical schools began using various tools to select candidates who possess strong soft skills such as communication skills, teamwork, empathy, critical thinking, ethical decision-making, interpersonal skills, and professionalism. The evaluative tools that were initially introduced included the personal statement, autobiographical sketch, short essays, and the traditional interview. Though the traditional interview is still used by many institutions, other interview formats have evolved and become increasingly popular. The following is a list of the formats you may encounter at your medical school interview:

- Traditional one-on-one or panel interview
- Group interview
- Multiple Mini Interview (MMI)
- Hybrid interview
- Modified Personal Interview (MPI)
- Virtual or video interview

We will take a close look at each of them in *Chapter V: 6 Types of Medical School Interviews*, noting how they are structured, who the evaluators are, and the rationale behind using them.

How reliable and valid are interviews for assessing applicants?

There is some evidence that interview assessments are *reliable*. That is to say, results are somewhat consistent across multiple tests over time. For example, research by Dahlin and colleagues (2012) shows that candidates who are selected by both their interview and academic performances, rather than their academic qualifications alone, perform better on future clinical examinations like the objective structured clinical examination (OSCE).

However, the validity of interview assessments has been called into question. Unlike the evaluation of hard skills in standardized tests, the evaluation of soft skills is qualitative and subjective. Therefore, regardless of which interview format is used, there will always be a question of how accurately applicants are being assessed. Many factors can influence applicants' interview ratings. Obviously, one of these is the difference between the competency of applicants themselves, but differences between the interviewers can also contribute to the variation in scores. These differences include, but are not limited to, inconsistent interviewer training, distinct interviewer experiences or backgrounds, and their longstanding (subconscious) biases. In particular, these biases can lead evaluators to make quick decisions and to selectively search for evidence to support their judgment, rather than evaluating all information equally and rating interviewees objectively. Ideally, differences between the applicants should account for most of the variance in their interview outcome, but in a study published in 1996, researchers Harasym and colleagues found that the variability between interviewers can account for up to 56% of the total variance in interview ratings! Therefore, even medical schools should be careful about the conclusions they draw from interviews alone.

Furthermore, two independent SortSmart studies on medical school admissions in the U.S. and Canada showed that *all* interview types used as admissions screening tools are more likely to select applicants from higher-income families. The results from U.S. schools are given in Figure 1.

The Wealthy are Most Represented

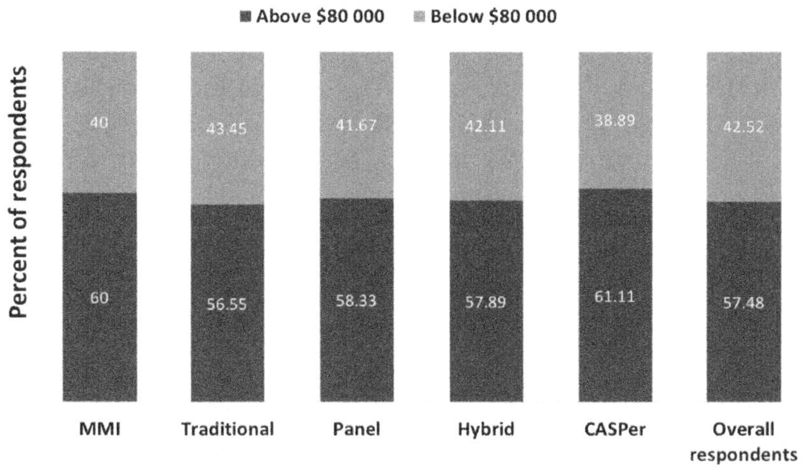

Figure 1. Students from families with an annual income greater than $80,000 represent the majority of successful applicants across all interview types. Printed with permission from SortSmart Candidate Selection Inc.

Figure 1 shows that candidates from families with annual incomes of $80,000 or more make up the majority of successful candidates across all interview formats and the CASPer test. This income distribution is concerning because it is not representative of the overall pool of applicants, in which there is no significant difference between the number of students from families earning below $80,000 per year and those from families earning above that threshold. It is also not representative of the American population, for which the median household income is approximately $60,000 per year, according to the U.S. Census Bureau. Though the connection is not certain, the bias from interviews and CASPer may stem from their use of situational judgment tests (SJTs) which also present the same bias (see below).

Situational Judgment Tests: Do they *really* work?

Situational judgment tests (SJTs) place applicants in hypothetical scenarios and allow interviewers to evaluate their approaches and behaviors. The assumption is that this method reveals applicants' true motivations and behavioral tendencies in real life situations. It is a methodology that has existed for decades and is currently used not only in MMIs and CASPer tests (MMI's online sister), but also in traditional, panel, hybrid, and even group interviews.

However, we have identified a number of problems with SJTs:

Problem #1

The use of hypothetical scenarios forces applicants to respond naturally to hypothetical situations. Students know that their response should be one that is socially acceptable. Therefore, instead of reflecting on what they *really* would do, applicants tend to say what they think is the 'right' answer. This means these tests might not be able to detect the true personality of applicants; they merely detect how attuned applicants are to social norms.

Problem #2

SJTs are biased against certain populations. Reports indicate that SJT scores tend to be lower for applicants with lower socioeconomic status, male applicants, and those from underrepresented minorities. We direct you to the following links for two of these studies:

https://www.ncbi.nlm.nih.gov/pubmed/26017355

https://www.ncbi.nlm.nih.gov/pubmed/28557950

Applicants from higher socioeconomic backgrounds are better at formulating socially acceptable responses due to their upbringing and socialization. Judging the appropriateness of a response to a very delicate or stressful hypothetical scenario can vary across cultures. These tests are singularly guided by accepted western cultural norms. This can pose significant challenges to non-native applicants, new immigrants, or those who are immersed in another culture. The diverse makeup of the population in the U.S., the U.K., Australia, and Canada, for example, makes this a significant barrier for applicants.

Problem #3

SJTs are often said to be 'immune to test preparation', a claim we find difficult to accept. Personal and professional behaviors are learned, not inherited; a parent, teacher, or coach can absolutely teach those skills to an individual. In fact, in *Chapter III: Top 2 Myths about Medical School Interview Preparation*, we discuss evidence showing that coaching can and does impact performance on these types of tests.

Problem #4

SJTs scores have not been shown to correlate with actual job behavior. The best correlation data to date is problematic in several ways: 1) It shows a correlation between test scores and future performance on medical licencing examinations, not job performance. 2) It is self-reported by the creators of the for-profit companies selling these products. 3) The correlation itself is weak, accounting for only about 16% of the variance in performance. Imagine going to a doctor who claimed to be able to make a correct diagnosis 16% of the time! Thus, we have no evidence showing that SJTs are a reliable way to evaluate which applicants will make great practicing professionals.

Problem #5

SJTs cannot measure each candidate's level of intrinsic motivation. Unlike test scores or grades, motivation directly impacts behavior. A motivated student is one who wants to improve themselves without outside direction or pressure and will work hard to become the best medical professional they can be. Furthermore, motivation is not correlated with gender, race, or socioeconomic status. Thus, it is a trait that should be evaluated, but isn't, and certainly not by SJTs.

Summary

Medical school admissions have evolved over time to enable the gatekeepers to gain insight into applicants' academic and professional suitability. On one hand, we haven't drifted from the principles of Schola Medica Salernitana: Serve others with both technical proficiency and interpersonal skills. On the other hand, we continue to fall short of this goal because of a lack of effective assessment tools for selecting medical students and professionals.

In this chapter, we outlined the history and rationale behind the use of interviews in the medical school admissions process and took a closer look at how useful (or not!) these interviews really are. Regardless, interviews are widely used as a screening tool, so you must still aim to do well on yours to gain admission to the medical school of your choice.

In the next chapters, we will delve into how preparation can help improve interview performance, distinguish between existing facts and myths, and take a closer look at the interview types and question types you will likely encounter at your interview.

CHAPTER II

Admissions Statistics and Why You Must ACE Your Medical School Interview

Each school uses your interview score in the way they see fit when deciding who is admitted and who is rejected. The best way to find out this information is to consult the official university admissions website or to contact the admissions office. Regardless, your interview performance is likely going to be a significant factor, if not *the* deciding factor, between you receiving an acceptance letter or a rejection letter.

In order to appreciate the importance of the interview in the overall admissions process, let's take two competitive Canadian medical schools as examples. At the University of Toronto's Faculty of Medicine, Canada's top-ranking medical school, approximately 600 applicants are invited to interview each year, but only half of these highly competitive individuals are admitted. At McMaster University's DeGroote Medical School, a mere 200 students are granted admission each year out of the 5000 people that apply. In this process, the MMI, McMaster's interview format of choice, accounts for a whopping 70% of the admissions score for each applicant. This gives you an idea of how heavily the interview portion of your application could be weighted. The same applies to U.S. medical schools.

Furthermore, previous years' admissions statistics from McMaster reveal that 1) many applicants with excellent MCAT and GPA scores do *not* gain admission, and 2) roughly 30% of accepted applicants had GPA and MCAT scores at or below the pooled average from all accepted applicants! You will notice that almost all schools using interviews as part of their admissions process accept students who have less than outstanding standardized tests or GPA scores. Thus, if you have competitive GPA and test scores, you can still get rejected from medical school if you perform poorly at your interview. On the other hand, even if you have below average GPA and test scores, you can still gain admission, but only if you ace your interview. We hope this makes it clear to you that you must prepare for and do well on your medical school interview. There are no shortcuts and no exceptions. If you are still skeptical, ask yourself this: Why would a school go to the trouble of using such a complicated, time-consuming, and expensive method, unless it was important?

Now that we have established the importance of the interview in the application, we can begin to lay the foundations for good interview preparation practices. As a first step, the next chapter will reveal and disprove two common myths about the process to help you avoid unnecessary setbacks.

Are you ready?

CHAPTER III

Top 2 Myths about Medical School Interview Preparation

The general conclusion you have probably come to by now is that the medical school interview is not going to be so easy. While that is true, we are going to do everything we can in the next few chapters to equip you with the tools necessary to succeed.

One thing that makes this process exceedingly difficult to navigate is the plethora of misinformation about how to prepare, which can set you off-course from your intended goals, in this case, acing your interview. That is why we have dedicated this chapter to dispelling two common myths about the preparation process so that you can avoid these pitfalls.

Myth #1: "There are no right or wrong answers."

This is a statement about interviews you might hear that sometimes even appears on official admissions websites. While it may sound plausible given the open-endedness of many interview questions, it simply cannot be true. If it were true, everyone would get accepted, regardless of their performance at their interview, which would make the entire exercise an extravagant waste of everyone's time. At best, this statement is dangerously misleading, causing many applicants to underprepare for and fail their interviews. In reality, although there are no *specific* right or wrong answers to the interview questions you will encounter, there are certainly appropriate and inappropriate answers. That is, there is a marked difference between a well-thought-out, mature, professional, and articulate response, and one that is immature, unprofessional, and disorganized. It is your job to put in the effort and time to learn how to do the former and avoid the latter. Otherwise, a rejection letter is as likely as the rising sun.

Myth #2: "You can't prepare in advance."

This is the most common and absurd myth about the medical school interview, one that is, sadly, also promoted on some official admissions websites. Medical interviews have been *claimed* to test personal and professional characteristics such as empathy, communication, and ethics, all of which are *learned* behaviors. Nobody is *born* with any of these.

You and other students who are participating in our interview preparation programs likely do not need to be convinced of this. Clearly, you have picked up this book and/or signed up for our programs because you believe there is something tangible you can do to improve your chances of success before walking into that interview room. Nevertheless, we thought it would still be helpful to break down this myth and look at some scientific proof showing that it is false.

First, consider the effectiveness of training on performance and level of success. We recently conducted a study to evaluate the effectiveness of our interview preparation program. The study included 29 randomly selected students with an upcoming medical school interview. A given student's baseline performance was the numeric score obtained from an expert's evaluation of their first realistic mock interview in BeMoMedInterview.com program. As part of the feedback for that interview, the student was coached by the expert who identified areas in need of improvement. Each student received 6 to 8 mock interviews followed by expert feedback, and the numeric scores from their final mock interviews were used to measure their improvement against the baseline. To avoid confounding factors that could interfere with our study, we used a double-blind method in which neither our students nor our consultants were aware that the study was being conducted until after its completion. The results are given in Figure 2.

Effect of Expert Training on Interview Practice Scores

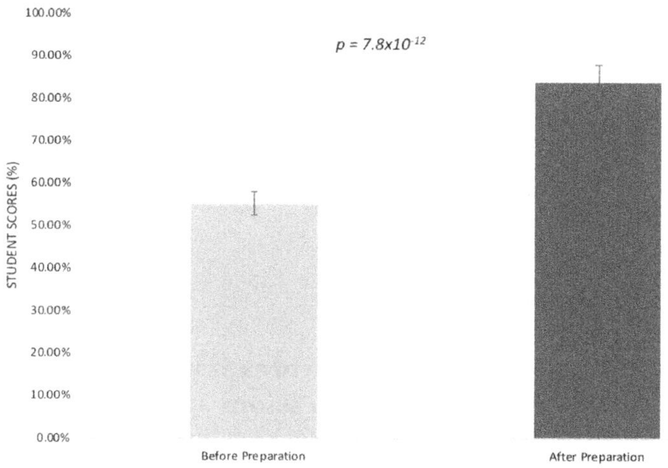

Figure 2. Students' interview practice scores improved by an average of 28.57% on interview simulations after 6 to 8 BeMo interview preparation sessions with expert feedback.

Before preparation, the students' average score was 55.17% (left bar). After preparation with experts, the students' average score was 83.74% (right bar). The small *p*-value indicates that the probability of this difference arising by chance is next to zero. Thus, we can confidently say that training works!

We additionally evaluated the effectiveness of our popular MMI Prep and CASPer Prep programs and found similar results. 44 students were included in the MMI study and their performance was evaluated after 6 to 8 sessions with mock interviews and expert feedback, while 24 students were included in the CASPer study and evaluated after only 3 sessions. The results are given in Figure 3.

Effect of Expert Training on MMI and CASPer Practice Scores

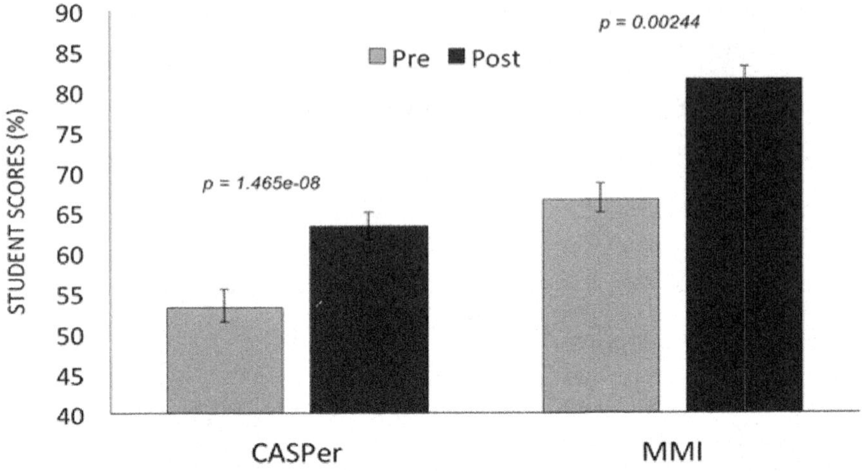

Figure 3. Applicants' MMI practice scores improved by 27% on average after 6 to 8 MMI preparation sessions and expert feedback with BeMo.

Figure 3 clearly shows a marked improvement in scores for both groups of students after training –27% for those training for MMI and 23% for those training for the CASPer test. When competing with thousands of other applicants, even a 1 to 2% increase in your interview score could set you apart, so an increase of more than 20% would almost certainly guarantee you an acceptance letter! Indeed, our interview preparation programs like those we tested in the studies above have an overall success rate of 93.5%, meaning that the vast majority of students who go through our programs gain acceptance into medical school. Therefore, we firmly believe in the power of practice! Myth busted.

Of course, there are also studies supporting the opposing view that interview preparation has no effect on performance. This is likely due to a fundamental difference in what we consider as practice. Studies that find no difference in performance often equate practice with reading over and trying sample questions without any feedback. Well, we absolutely agree that this kind of preparation will not improve your interview performance! At BeMo, we have always said that practice does not make perfect, practice makes permanent. It is only *perfect* practice that makes perfect. That means you only get better at interviewing if you practice using realistic simulations followed by expert feedback. You need an interview coach to tell you what you are doing well, what you are doing poorly, and how to do better. Ideally, you would receive this kind of expert feedback throughout your interview preparation to keep you on track and make sure you are actually improving. That is the BeMo difference!

Another reason for rejecting this myth, as we have already discussed in a previous chapter, is that medical interviews are biased towards a certain group of people who have been immersed in 'preparation' for these tests their whole lives – those who come from families with higher socioeconomic status. People from wealthier families learn to *display* these skills as part of their upbringing through grooming and specific opportunities for socialization. We showed this with results from an independent SortSmart study on the income of admitted students in U.S. medical schools by interview type (see Figure 1). In Figure 4 below, we provide a further breakdown of the income brackets of the students from that study.

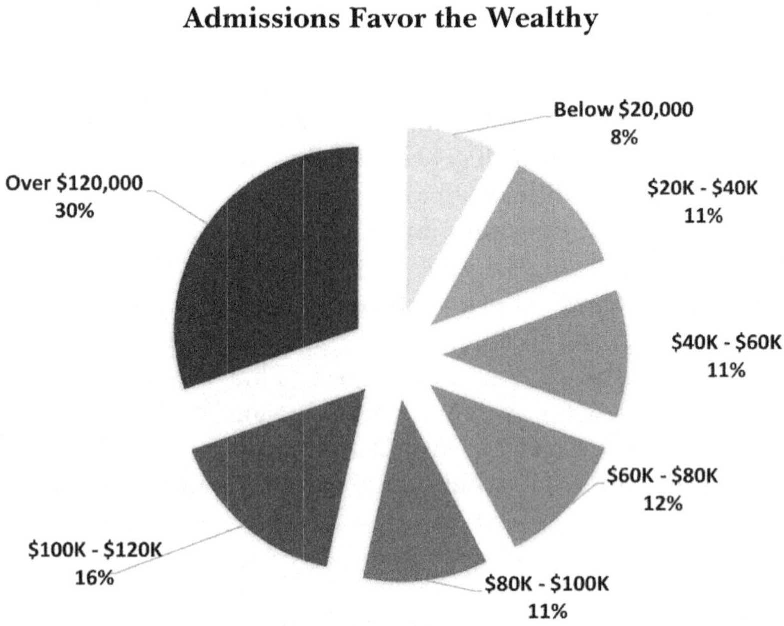

Figure 4. 69% of medical school students and residents reported household income of over $60k/year at the time of application. Printed by permission from SortSmart Candidate Selection Inc.

Figure 4 shows that more than two thirds of admitted students come from families with annual incomes more than the median U.S. household income of $60K. Furthermore, almost a third of all admitted students from this study come from families with an annual household income of $120K, which is double the median household income.

Now, you may be wondering if the admissions bias highlighted above could be due to the fact that applicants from wealthier families are more likely to use (evidently effective) medical school preparation programs and are therefore more successful at gaining admission. Therefore, as part of the two independent SortSmart studies, we also compared the likelihood of applicants from high- and low-income families to use paid preparatory programs. Figure 5 shows these results grouped by the type of program.

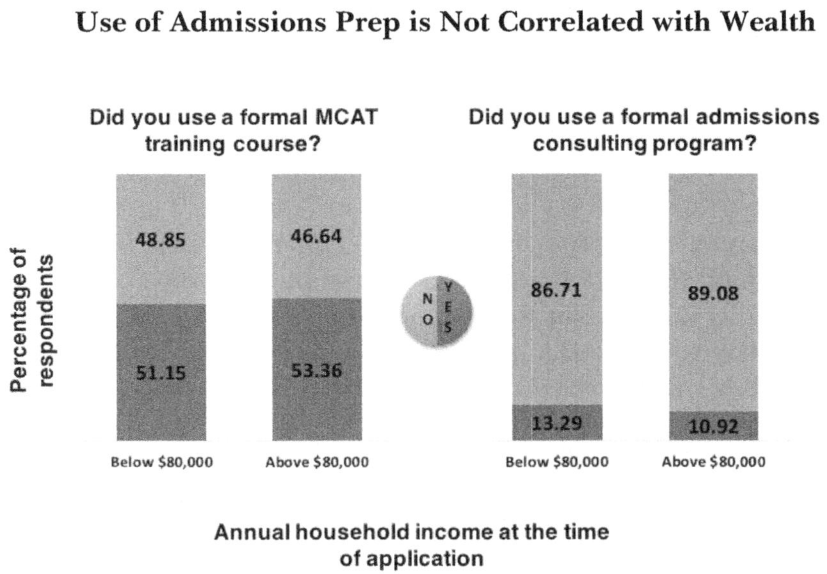

Figure 5. Wealth does not correlate with the likelihood of using admissions preparation services. Printed with permission from SortSmart Candidate Selection Inc.

As you can see in Figure 5, there is no significant difference in the proportion of applicants from different income backgrounds who had used training programs for either the MCAT or for general admissions consultation. These results show that students from lower-income families are just as likely as those from higher-income families to use and pay for professional training. This makes sense given that the cost of these services, including ours, is a mere fraction of the combined cost of the application, travel to and from the interview site, and of course, tuition for professional school.

Therefore, the bias in the admissions process cannot be due to greater access to admissions preparation programs. Instead, the screening tools used in the admissions process must themselves be held to account. In fact, 94% of the medical students and residents from our studies are in support of using new admissions screening tools that are transparent and more accurate measures of applicant traits and intrinsic motivation.

If you were not skeptical of the claim that you cannot prepare for an interview, we hope that we have convinced you of its absurdity. While we do not know why some admissions offices are making these claims, the evidence clearly points in the opposite direction. On one hand, we showed that with proper training and expert feedback, our students' performance on interviews does improve. On the other hand, we have also shown you that the screening tools used by medical schools actually favor those who have had ample opportunity to 'train' for these tests throughout their upbringing. Knowing this, we, as a company, have been working tirelessly to empower our students with the tools they need to succeed, no matter what their socioeconomic background. A significant portion of our revenue is cycled back and used for research and development of a new admissions screening tools that meet our standards of fairness and scientific integrity. Regardless of what the claims are and who is promoting this information, we will continue to advocate for on behalf of all students and work toward realizing bias-free admissions.

Now, it is up to you how you want to move forward. You can choose to believe those myths and do nothing to prepare for your imminent medical school interview, or you can reject these falsities and get to work before it's too late! We hope you have chosen the latter because we are eager continue sharing what we know with you to help you succeed. In the next chapter, we will be discussing the most common mistakes applicants make on their interviews to help you avoid making the same errors.

CHAPTER IV

5 Common Errors Made in Medical School Interviews

Now that we have debunked the myths about interview preparation, let's take a look at the common mistakes applicants make when they prepare for their interviews and during the interview itself. It is important that you understand why these errors may hurt your performance and what you can do to avoid making them yourself.

In this chapter, we focus on 5 errors: lack of preparation, poor delivery, lack of structure, red flags, and inappropriate attire. As we discuss each one, evaluate your own interview practice thus far and think about whether you have made these mistakes yourself.

1. Lack of Preparation

Applicants often neglect the importance of preparation. This mistake is commonly made by those who feel confident about their interview skills, whether this confidence is well-grounded or not. It is also made by individuals with many interview invitations as they tend to become overly confident about their chances of admission, forgetting that they still need to perform well at each interview.

As we have established, the interview is an extremely important part of the admissions process. Think of your interview as a behavioral test. It takes a long time to develop new habits and curb undesirable behaviors. Additionally, each interview you participate in will differ in content and perhaps also style. Thus, preparing for each individual interview in advance is absolutely necessary. In our experience, it takes at least 6 to 8 weeks to fully prepare for a medical school interview.

Interviewers value, among other things, your interest in their particular program. One way to demonstrate this is through *preparedness*, which will be apparent if your responses are thoughtful and well-articulated. With that in mind, research each individual program you will be interviewing for. Your ability to connect with a school's mission statement and teaching methods may make a lasting impression on the interviewers, further increasing your chances of admission.

See Point 3 below for how to structure your interview preparation to make the most effective use of your time.

2. Poor Delivery

Confident, smooth, and well-articulated speech makes a great impression on the interviewer regardless of the content. We are not underestimating the importance of comprehensive and in-depth answers, but the truth is that a lot of what admissions committees look at is delivery. You can have a wonderful argument to make, but if it is interrupted with pauses, filler words, or repetition, your interviewer will not even take notice of what you are saying.

It is therefore important to deliver your structured answers confidently and concisely. Admissions committees seek applicants who are both eloquent and informative in their responses. By delivering your strong arguments in a structured way, you will not only win the case, but also leave a lasting impression on the interviewer. It will help the interviewer follow your thought process and better understand your logic. The following are some aspects to consider with regards to delivery.

Introductions & Conclusions

A common mistake observed among applicants is that they do not even acknowledge the interviewer in the room. However, the way you introduce yourself and conclude your interview will also play a significant role in how the interviewer views you as an applicant. The introduction is the first time the interviewer gets to know you and your professional etiquette. A polite, professional greeting and introduction go a long way in making that initial positive impression on the interviewer. Therefore, it is absolutely crucial to address the interviewer with their name and professional title at the beginning of your interview.

Another common mistake is that the applicants tend to spend a long time introducing themselves and talking about their stories before the interview even begins. Although the introduction is very important, it should be concise and to-the-point. Similarly, the conclusion is the time to nicely and concisely thank the interviewer by name and express your appreciation for their time.

The following is an example of a proper introduction:

Applicant: Good morning, I'm John. Who do I have the pleasure of speaking to today? (Once the interviewer has stated his/her name, acknowledge him/her by name.) Dr. Johnson, it is a pleasure to meet you. Thank you for the opportunity to interview for your program.

The following is an example of a proper conclusion:

Applicant: Thank you, Dr. Johnson, for the time spent with me today. It was a pleasure to meet you and discuss my answers with you today. Once again, I would like to express my interest in this school/program, and I hope to see you in the future.

Filler Words

Another commonly observed mistake during interviews is the excessive use of filler words and pauses. Each individual may use a slightly different set of filler words, but some common ones include "um", "uh", and "like". The use of filler words is habitual for some people, while for others it could be induced by contextual factors like added stress, lack of preparation, and poor vocabulary on a given topic. Some filler words can be eliminated relatively quickly, but others may require more time. Regardless, reducing the number of filler words and pauses requires great initiative and self-awareness. Have your speech evaluated by a professional interviewer or at least someone who can point out which filler words you are using and when you tend to use them. The next step is to practice. You can record yourself and self-monitor your speech, or practice with a friend or family member and ask them to restart the conversation every time you use a filler word unnecessarily. This will make you more cognizant of your mistakes and help you to minimizing your use of filler words and/or pauses gradually.

Lack of Enthusiasm

Applicants often underestimate the importance of showing enthusiasm for the program they are interviewing for. They may arrive late at the interview site, show obvious signs of fatigue, and have an uncaring attitude. However, it is important to show enthusiasm from beginning to end during your interview. Arrive on-time. Create a positive atmosphere during the introduction as this will enable you to open up further and fully demonstrate your personality. Otherwise, the interviewer will be less likely to engage with you and will only have a dry conversation with you that will not set you apart from other candidates. Your level of enthusiasm can also determine whether the interviewer believes you will fit into their particular school and whether you reflect their mission statement. The interviewers will remember you by the way you carry and present yourself during that specific interaction. Remember to smile and express excitement about being there to communicate to them that their program is your number-one choice. As discussed above, it is also important to show appreciation for the people who interview you, so be sure to thank them for their time. The enthusiasm and professionalism you demonstrate during your interview go a long way to show that you care about the opportunity.

3. Lack of Structure

As previously discussed, the ability to interview well is acquired, not inherited. As part of this skill, you must learn to structure your answers so that your ideas come through the way you intended. As important as it is for you to express your point of view, it is also crucial for you to show your analytical skills and objectivity when tackling each issue. The general rule of thumb is to refrain from jumping to conclusions and lay out your arguments before presenting your opinions and proposing solutions. You do not want to come off as judgmental or biased as a result of poor structure. Of course, being able to progress through your ideas logically will also help the interviewer follow your answer and understand your points. The specific structures and strategies to use for different question types will be covered in detail in *Chapter VII: Proven Strategies to Approach and Ace Any Medical School Interview Question*.

Structure is not only important in your answers, but also in your preparation. In order to prepare for the most important interview in your professional career thus far, you will spend hours going over sample questions and scenarios. However, many applicants do not set out with clear objectives, are unable to identify their strengths and weaknesses, and therefore are unable to formulate a plan of action and monitor their own progress. To approach the task more systematically, have a third party evaluate your responses at different points in your preparation, and practice based on the feedback you get. If that third party is a well-trained expert, they will also be able to point out when you are not directly addressing the question, or ways in which you can address the question better. You can then target the areas that need improvement, whether that be your delivery, content, or organization. This is how you will make the best use of the time you dedicate to interview preparation and ensure that you are making good progress toward your interview goals. Also try to practice with people you don't know well so your approach to the questions is more professional and less colloquial. Introducing uncertainty to the process is extremely important during preparation as it pushes you to deliver your answers under stress, mimicking the actual interview.

Using a structured, step-by-step approach during practice will raise your confidence level, increase your vocabulary, and improve your overall delivery. Of course, there will be times where the interviewers will still surprise you with questions you were not expecting, but the previous preparation you have done will help you remain calm and think on your feet.

4. Red Flags

Among the many mistakes you could make, only 'red flags' are truly detrimental to your application score. Therefore, it is crucial for you to avoid any potential red flags during the entire application process, including at your interview. Below, we will take a look at three major red flags: dishonesty about your application or experiences, lack of ethical judgment, and unprofessional appearance.

A common red flag is when applicants present answers that are inconsistent with their CV or primary application. Whether the applicant listed an experience just to pad their CV, or they gave an inaccurate description of their level of involvement, this lack of transparency can and will negatively influence their chances of admission. All admission committees seek and respect applicants who are, first and foremost, honest. Therefore, while you prepare for your interview, ensure that your answers are not only well-structured, but also a true reflection of you and your experiences.

Another red flag is the lack of ethical judgment. This could happen if you omit or misidentify the pressing issue in an interview scenario, which could lead you to make a poor ethical judgment in your answer. It is important to correctly identify the most pressing concern in any situation, show that you are non-judgmental and considerate of others' perspectives, not just your own. In this way, you can demonstrate to the interviewers that you are able to respond ethically in difficult situations in your future profession.

The third red flag is inappropriate attire. Since this is considered a significant red flag, it will be discussed as a separate point below.

5. Inappropriate Attire or Appearance

Professional attire and presentation during interviews are often underemphasized, but having a professional appearance goes hand-in-hand with being professional in speech. When either of these is lacking, you paint yourself as an unprepared and potentially disrespectful applicant, one that the interviewers will find difficult to value. Therefore, professional attire and appearance will be important elements to your success. Remember that medicine is still a conservative profession. You want to stand out because of your personality and outstanding communication and argumentative skills, not because of your attire. For detailed guidance on how to dress appropriately, see *Chapter IX: What to Wear, What to Say, and How to Communicate Non-verbally During Your Interview*.

Now that we have discussed the most common errors applicants make during their interviews and how you can avoid them, we can begin to discuss the medical school interview itself. This will be the contents of the next few chapters. We begin in the next chapter with the types of interviews you may encounter and the proven strategies to help you ace them.

CHAPTER V

6 Types of Medical School Interviews

As you may recall in *Chapter I: What is a Medical School Interview?*, we discussed how interviews have evolved. One thing to note is that interview formats continue to develop, and though programs often use one particular format, they could also change it each year. For this reason, it is important for you to become familiar with all interview formats. This chapter breaks down the types of interviews you may encounter on your application journey to give you a good understanding of their structure, why each is used, who you will be interviewed by, and what these interviewers are looking for. At various points throughout this chapter, we mention question types that are common in each of these interview formats. These will be defined and discussed in detail in *Chapter VII: Proven Strategies to Approach and Ace Any Medical School Interview Question*.

In any type of interview, the following three components will be factored into your score:

Content:

What you say is obviously crucial! You will likely be evaluated on the validity of your ideas, the strength of your arguments and examples, the lessons you propose to have learned from your personal experiences, the justifications for actions you propose to take, and so forth.

Delivery:

Of course, interviewers will also consider how well you communicate the content of your answer. They want to see that you can present your points in an organized and concise way, without rambling or going on tangents, and with minimal filler words. As a physician, you will have to relay complex information to patients and colleagues in a way that can be easily understood. Therefore, delivery in both verbal and written communication is key!

Suitability for the profession:

Based on what you say and how you say it, the interviewers will make a judgment on how well suited you are for both the profession of medicine and also their particular program. Have you demonstrated that you are a mature and thoughtful individual who works well with others? Did you show leadership and advocacy skills? Do your values align with those of the school or program? Educate yourself before your interview by researching the school thoroughly and reading about their curriculum and mission. You will then know what types of qualities they are looking for.

Keep these three criteria in mind as you prepare for any type of interview. To do well, you must be able to think like the interviewer and evaluate your own performance against these measures.

1. Traditional Interviews: One-on-One or Panel

What is a traditional interview?

In a traditional interview, a single candidate is interviewed by up to four panelists. Your program may have just one traditional interview, or it could have two or three one-on-one interviews where you move from room to room. During your interview, you will be asked a series of questions, either by one interviewer (one-on-one) or in turn by the panelists. Each individual's overall impression of your performance will form the basis of the recommendation they make to the admissions committee.

Traditional interviews tend to be short, lasting 20 minutes on average. This means you must practice making your answers in-depth, yet concise!

Your interview can be *open*- or *closed*-file. An open interview means the interviewers have seen some or all of your application documents, including your transcript, essays, and reference letters, and are free to ask you about anything on your application during the interview. If you are told your interview will be open, or if it is not explicitly stated which type of interview it will be, you should review your application documents in detail prior to the interview to prepare for questions that pertain to the experiences you discussed therein. In contrast, a closed interview means the interviewers know nothing about you but your name. The questions you are asked in this interview will therefore not be tailored to your profile. However, the interviewers may still ask you to elaborate on the experiences and ideas you bring up in your answers, so you should be prepared to discuss them in more detail.

Most traditional interviews will focus on asking personal or program-based questions about your past experiences, why you are pursuing medicine, and why you are interested in their program. However, they can still ask for your views about current issues, give you scenarios to respond to, or anything else! You must therefore be prepared to answer any type of question at your interview.

A traditional interview is usually not rigidly structured. If the interviewers have pre-prepared questions, you can expect between 7 to 10 questions. Otherwise, the interview may be conversational, and the interviewers will follow your lead and see where the conversation goes before deciding which questions to ask you. For this reason, a traditional interview may not have a strict scoring rubric or a scoring sheet. The interviewer may be asked to simply share their thoughts about you with the admissions committee after your interview.

Who are your interviewers?

A traditional interview is typically conducted by a representative of the medical school faculty, current medical students, and residents. If there are multiple interviewers in a panel, one of them may also be a community representative or an allied health professional. The role of the community member may be to assess how well you communicate with someone who has no medical background.

Why is this format used?

Traditional interviews are still used because they are inexpensive, straightforward, and flexible. Being less structured, it is far easier for the interviewers to follow up on any points you make that need clarification or address potential red flags in your CV or your answers. Traditional interviewers are typically friendly and collegial, and hence can put the applicant at ease and get them to open up about their story and experiences.

2. Group Interviews

What is a group interview?

A group interview is one that is conducted with anywhere from 2 to 10 candidates simultaneously. Candidates may be asked to discuss a topic or question with one another, or they may be given a group task or problem to tackle. At your interview, for example, you and other candidates could be asked to discuss policies surrounding the legalization of recreational marijuana, or you could be given an MMI-style ethical scenario and asked how you would respond to it as a group.

While most schools do not rely exclusively on group interviews, many schools have incorporated them as a component in their interviews. You may find yourself in a group station either after completing a traditional interview or in the middle of your MMI!

Who are your interviewers?

Similar to traditional interviews, the interviewer may be a faculty member, current student, or a community member. Interestingly, in a group interview, you may have very little interaction with the interviewer. The interviewer may facilitate the discussion, or they may simply stand to the side and observe the interactions going on between group members. Even if their interaction with the group is minimal, be aware that they are paying close attention to everything that is said and done!

Why is this format used?

Medicine is a heavily collaborative field; few physicians work in isolation. Typically, physicians work in clinics and hospitals where they interact with colleagues and patients every day. Thus, medical schools need to know that you can thrive in group settings, especially under time pressure.

What does success look like in group settings? Doing well on a group interview or a group station does not mean you overpower your fellow applicants. Rather, you must respectfully and professionally interact with them, seek their input, validate their thoughts and feelings, and collaborate on solutions. You must ensure that while you make your opinion heard, you are also allowing others to speak. Do not fall into the trap of treating a group station like a competition where you must outperform everyone else. View it instead as a group challenge that you must overcome together using communication and teamwork.

3. Multiple Mini Interviews (MMI)

What is the MMI?

The famous and much-feared Multiple Mini Interview, or MMI, was developed at McMaster University and has slowly, but surely, spread to medical schools and other professional programs around the world.

Unlike traditional interviews, where the same interviewer or panel asks all the questions, an MMI consists of 8 to12 stations, each with a different interviewer. At each station, you, the candidate, have 1.5 to 2 minutes to read and think about the question outside the room, and 4 to 8 minutes inside the room to respond to the prompt as well as any follow-up questions the interviewer may have. Once this time is up, you move to the next station, and the cycle repeats until you have cycled through all the stations.

All MMIs are necessarily closed interviews with a standard scoring protocol. The interviewer at each station will score you on a scale of 1 (poor) to 10 (outstanding) based on a) the strength of your arguments and content, b) your communication skills and the delivery of your answer, and c) your suitability for the profession of medicine. Note that your score for a given station is *relative* to that of other candidates for the same station. Thus, you can still get a relatively high score at a station that you found difficult if it was difficult for everyone.

Although scenario- or situational-type questions are commonly asked on MMIs, you can expect to be asked any question type at an MMI station, so be prepared for all possible question types.

Who are your interviewers?

MMI assessors are a mix of faculty members, current students and residents, and community members or allied health professionals. Each assessor will be sitting at one station, and they will score all 8 to12 candidates who come through that station in a given cycle.

Keep in mind that MMI assessors are trained not to give any positive or negative feedback to interview candidates. They may have minimal interaction with you during your station and may simply sit and look at you, without smiling or acknowledging your thoughts. They are instructed to not give any sort of feedback, either through their expressions or words, as they are aiming to not influence your answer in any way. Do not be thrown off by this or feel that your answer is not strong because the interviewer is expressionless. This is normal for the MMI!

Why is this format used?

MMIs allow programs to interview a large number of applicants in a much shorter period of time, making it a more efficient process. The interviewers also know nothing about you, which may eliminate some of the bias inherent in open interviews where they may be aware of your grades or which undergraduate degree you have. You will receive independent scores from at least 8 people, which is a larger number of assessors than traditional interviews allow. This means doing poorly at one station need not affect your score at the next station, and you can still do very well overall. This scoring method can also remove the candidate ordering bias that is of concern for medical schools using other interview formats. Since candidates rotate through the stations and no one is always first or always last, any biases the interviewers have when scoring earlier vs. later candidates is cancelled out when the scores are pooled.

Although it is impossible to completely eliminate human biases in the interview process, the promise of a more objective and efficient way of interviewing applicants has made the MMI the interview format of choice for many medical schools worldwide.

For more information on the MMI, including research about its validity and reliability, we refer you to our book *BeMo's Ultimate Guide to the Multiple Mini Interview (MMI).*

4. Hybrid Interviews

What is a hybrid interview?

A hybrid interview is one that combines elements of both a traditional interview and an MMI. Typically, this will consist of an MMI with fewer stations, preceded or followed by one or more traditional one-on-one or panel interviews. For example, you may have a 5-station MMI, followed by a 10-minute panel interview with two panelists. The format and scoring protocols of each portion of the interview follows what we have outlined above. Keep in mind that while the MMI will always be closed, the traditional portion of a hybrid interview can be closed or open.

Who are your interviewers?

You will have the same mix of interviewers mentioned above: faculty members, current trainees, and community members.

Why is this format used?

Quite simply, some programs want the combined benefits of both interview formats. They want to have the promised objectivity of the MMI alongside the more collegial and personal traditional interview in the hopes of getting a fuller picture of each applicant.

5. Modified Personal Interviews (MPI)

What is an MPI?

The Modified Personal Interview (MPI) is used by the University of Toronto's medical school. Candidates cycle through four stations, and they typically have 10 to 12 minutes in each room to answer 3 to 5 questions posed by the interviewer. This interview style has traditionally been open-file, and each interviewer will have formulated questions for the candidates based on the contents of their application.

The interviewers rate each candidate on four aspects: maturity, communication skills, interpersonal skills, and one attribute unique to each candidate. This fourth skill may relate to the candidate's ability to work in a team setting, their overall vision and expectations, their ability to multitask or solve complex problems, their adaptability and introspection, and so forth. For each of the four components, candidates will be ranked on a scale of 1 (poor) to 5 (outstanding), adding up to a total score of 20.

The MPI, as implied in the name, focuses on personal questions that ask about why you are pursuing medicine, your past experiences, as well as your approach to situations involving conflict resolution, teamwork, or leadership. However, keep in mind that you can still be asked any question type on the MPI, so be prepared!

Who are your interviewers?

Like the interview styles outlined above, MPI interviewers are faculty members, current students or residents, or people outside the profession who are part of the admissions committee, such as allied health professionals.

Why is this format used?

The MPI is designed to identify personal qualities and characteristics that the program believes make you a strong candidate and future physician. By combining some elements of a traditional interview (personal questions and open-file) and the MMI (different rooms and independent assessors), the University of Toronto hopes to combine the benefits of both interview types.

6. Virtual or Video Interviews

What is a virtual or video interview?

More recently, some universities have opted for an online, virtual or video interview. In this interview format, there are no live interviewers; candidates simply record themselves responding to pre-prepared question prompts. The number of questions, type of questions used, and how much time you have to respond to each are program-specific. However, the logistics remain fairly consistent. Usually, you would receive instructions and login details to an online interviewing platform from the school. While some schools allow you to schedule your own interview within a given timeframe, others would simply assign you a time slot or give you a timeframe to submit your responses. Since technical problems are common, some schools also allow you to practice using their online platform before doing the real interview. Once all the responses have been recorded and uploaded, they are sent to the reviewers for scoring. It may be the case that all the responses of an applicant are reviewed by the same person or group of people. However, it is more likely that each response is independently evaluated by a different person, much like the MMI or MPI.

Who are your interviewers?

There are no live interviewers, but the group of people scoring these video responses will be comprised of faculty members, current students and residents, and other members of the admissions committee, such as allied professionals. On this aspect, virtual interviews are not different from live interviews.

Why is this format used?

Such interviews are utilized for a number of reasons, some to do with efficiency, and others to do with eliminating bias. First, this interview format can drastically speed up the interview process since a large number of interviews can be conducted simultaneously, and responses from all applicants can be collected within a fairly short period of time. From the candidate's perspective, this interview format allows them to participate in the interview from the comfort of their own home. More importantly, it saves them the time and cost of travelling to an interview site, thus removing some potential barriers that make on-site interviews difficult or even impossible for some individuals. Furthermore, candidates' responses cannot be influenced by feedback, verbal or non-verbal, from an interviewer, so virtual interviews can also be effective in eliminating interviewer biases.

We hope that this breakdown of the interview formats has given you some insight into how to prepare for your own interview. Throughout this chapter, we also hinted at some of the question types you can expect to encounter. These will be discussed systematically and in greater detail in the next chapter.

CHAPTER VI

Pre-mortem: 18 Proven Strategies to Prepare for and Ace Any Medical School Interview

As emphasized in previous chapters, you *can* and absolutely *must* prepare for medical school interviews in advance. All human behavior is learned, and just like for any exam, there are specific strategies you can use to ace your interview. This chapter will provide you with an overview of the general interviewing strategies we teach students in our sought-after medical school interview preparation programs. We know from experience that they work, and they work consistently. Therefore, take the time to read this chapter multiple times before you move on, and keep referring to these instructions as you prepare for your actual interview. Many of them will be expanded in later chapters.

1. Think like the interviewers.

Recall that in the previous chapter, we shared the 3 main aspects you will be scored on in any interview format. These are the following:

a) Communication skills (how well you delivered your answer)
b) Content (your ideas and arguments)
c) Your suitability for the medical profession and for the specific program

In order to think like the interviewer, imagine you are on the other side of the process and you are given a scoring sheet. For each response you give, ask yourself how well it measures on each of these aspects and how you might adjust your response to achieve a better score. One of the many things we encourage our students to do in our interview preparation programs is to reflect on their own performance, evaluate themselves, and monitor their own progress in between sessions. We even ask them to create new sample questions to answer, and in doing so, understand what interviewers are looking for. In order to do well in an interview, it is important to be acutely aware of the criteria on which your evaluation will be based.

2. Learn to manage your stress.

One of the most common reasons applicants do poorly on their interviews is their inability to control their stress level. Nothing is worse than feeling so nervous that you are unable to formulate a coherent response. Among other things, poor delivery would certainly have a negative impact on the interviewer's evaluation of your communication skills. Remember also that medicine is a stressful profession, and interviewers need to see that you can manage it well.

This point is so important that we have dedicated an entire chapter to long-term and short-term strategies for stress management. Stay tuned for that in *Chapter X: How to Manage Stress*!

3. Don't rush to answer.

Candidates often feel as though they must begin answering the prompt as soon as they enter the MMI station or as soon as the interviewer finishes asking the question. This is never the case! Make sure you take your time to read and/or think over each question at least *twice* before answering.

For an MMI, you will have time outside the room to gather your thoughts and organize your answer. Since, in practice, an organized and concise response should take no longer than 3 to 4 minutes to execute, you might be able to afford an extra minute or two outside the room to make sure you understand the question even after the buzzer sounds. If you do enter the room late, make sure you briefly apologize for the delay, and explain that you wanted a bit more time to gather your thoughts before delivering your response. This will actually put you ahead of your competition, because it shows your ability to think carefully and deliberate, even in high-stress situations.

If your question is given to you verbally, as would be the case in a traditional interview, it would be perfectly acceptable to say, "May I please have a moment to organize my thoughts?" Then, take the time to think about what you want to say and how you want to say it. If you rush, you are more likely to miss key information, your answer will be less organized, and you may even give a biased response.

4. Use the *primacy effect* to your advantage.

It goes without saying that once you enter the room, you must smile, greet the interviewer by name, introduce yourself, and when appropriate, shake hands – all before delivering your response. This is something candidates often miss because they are too nervous to remember that the interview is also a test of their professionalism. Interestingly, your interviewer is more likely to remember the first moments of your interaction compared to everything that follows. This is a well-documented phenomenon in psychology called the *primacy effect*, which is the tendency for people to recall earlier events better than later events. Thus, when you are being evaluated, nuances at the beginning of your interview can make a significant difference!

5. Master your non-verbal communication skills.

There is ample evidence in the literature that non-verbal cues make up for a large portion of human communication compared to verbal communication. This includes using eye contact, facial expressions, and posture.

Eye contact:

We are hardwired to look into other people's eyes because they are an important mode of communication. For example, infants, who are unable to talk, are able to communicate with their parents with something as simple as eye contact. This is why you may have seen a crying infant going into an almost instant calm after making eye contact with his or her mother. During your interview, maintain eye contact about 70% of the time to communicate confidence to the interviewers. This also shows that you are being respectful and paying close attention. Remember not to stare intently, as this can create a tense atmosphere and make the interviewer feel uncomfortable. If maintaining eye contact does not come naturally to you, practice!

Facial expressions:

Humans are hard-wired to detect happiness, sadness, fear, surprise, disgust, anger, and so forth simply by reading the micro-expressions on each other's faces. Your goal, as an interviewee, is to communicate specific emotions at appropriate moments. When you enter the interview room, for example, you need to show that you are excited and happy to be there, even though you might actually feel anxious at first. Your facial expression should differ when you are sharing a positive experience versus a negative one, and when you are discussing a vulnerable party versus a party with malicious intent. If you are in an acting station and the actor reveals that they just received news of their mother's passing, you must reflect their sorrow and show genuine concern. For any hypothetical situation, try to immerse yourself in the scenario as much as possible and respond as you would if it were actually happening. That way, the emotions you bring and the facial expressions that come with them will be genuine.

Genuine smile:

There is a difference between a fake smile and a genuine smile. A genuine smile induces wrinkles around the eyes, whereas a fake one does not, and humans are exceptionally good at distinguishing the two at a subconscious level. If your smile is fake, you appear untrustworthy to the interviewer, but if you smile with your mouth and your eyes, you convey the kind of charisma and emotional generosity that draws people in and makes you stand out in their memories. Rather than putting on a fake 'genuine smile', think about the positive aspects of your interview, the prospect of attending medical school, or any other happy thoughts that would help you bring a genuine smile to your interview.

Body posture:

Your body language can say a lot about you, without you ever saying a word. When you are interacting with someone, whether it be an interviewer, an actor, or another applicant, make sure you are standing in front of them at a slight angle. Standing behind someone can increase their anxiety because they cannot anticipate what you are going to do if they cannot see you, but standing directly in front of them may be interpreted as confrontational. Make sure you are standing or sitting at an appropriate distance from others. If you are too close, it may seem intimidating and you may be invading their space, but if you are too far, you may seem too distant, aloof, or cold. Also be aware of what you are doing with your hands and arms. Standing with your hands on your hips can convey aggression and crossing your arms signifies defensiveness or insecurity. If you are sitting down while listening to someone, lean slightly forward to show focus and interest.

If you found these helpful, stay tuned for *Chapter IX: What to Wear, What to Say, and How to Communicate Non-verbally during Your Interview* where we will address more points about non-verbal communication!

6. Identify the most pressing issue.

Your first task after reading or hearing an interview question is to figure out the most pressing issue. Generally, this is the well-being of those under your care or of a vulnerable group or party, such as patients, students, children, and so forth. You must ask yourself whether someone's safety is at stake or if there are larger implications for society as a whole. If you are a doctor, your primary concern is for the well-being of your patients. If you are a teacher, it is the well-being of your students. If you are the captain of an oil tanker, and the tanker is leaking, the most pressing issue is the well-being of your crew and the immediate and long-term impact of an oil leak on the environment. Many scenarios will include distracting information or multiple perspectives. If there are multiple issues or multiple vulnerable parties, if may even be necessary for you to prioritize one or some over others after you have identified them. Identifying the pressing issue is especially important for scenario questions, but it may be useful for policy-related questions as well. Moreover, your ability to quickly and accurately identify the pressing issue comes with practice.

7. Always remain non-judgmental.

Whether you are exploring a controversial issue or discussing how you would handle a situation involving the wrong-doing or ignorance of others, you must remain non-judgmental. For questions about controversial issues, do not prematurely dismiss the reasoning and arguments from either side. Explore both sides of the argument without bias, and only state your own views after weighing both pros and cons. For scenario questions, do not assume that the other party is aware of their actions, has control over what they did, or has malintent. If you are in a position of power, do not assume that the other individual knows less than you or that you are necessarily right. A professional always reserves judgment and holds off on acting until they have fully assessed the situation.

8. Gather all the facts. Don't make any assumptions.

Interview questions are often intentionally missing key information. The interviewers are interested to see if you are going identify what is missing and gather all the facts first or make a hasty judgment of the situation and respond inappropriately. Let's assume in an acting question, the actor playing your friend, Tony, tells you that a man who might be intoxicated is walking to their car to drive away. You might be inclined to react by stopping the man immediately. However, it is important to take a step back and gather information by asking the right questions. Why does Tony think the man person is intoxicated? If it's because he smelled alcohol in the man's breath as he walked past, how do we know it isn't because he's diabetic and what Tony smelled was ketoacidosis? What if the man is indeed drunk, but he is simply going to grab something from his car? You simply don't know until you gather all the facts.

Keep in mind, if gathering facts involves discussing a sensitive topic with another individual, you must explicitly mention it will be a *private* conversation. As a professional, you never want to embarrass the person in front of others unless it is absolutely unavoidable. If you are describing your approach rather than acting it out, you may also want to make clear to the interviewer that you are approaching the conversation calmly, in a non-confrontational manner, and that you would want to maintain a neutral, friendly tone to avoid escalating the situation. If you do not make this clear, the interviewer will be free to assume your demeanor however they deem appropriate. That is too significant a factor to leave unaddressed when your communication skills are being evaluated. Just as you don't want to make assumptions in your response, you also don't want to give the interviewer room to make assumptions about your behavior in a delicate situation.

9. Figure out who is directly or indirectly involved.

As a future professional, you need to understand that real-life situations impact not only those directly involved in the situation, but also others on the periphery. Let's say you are about to fire the assistant coach of your college basketball team for professional misconduct. You, the coach, and the rest of the team are directly involved, but the college, the college basketball community, and the coach's family will also be impacted by your actions. Demonstrating awareness of the complexities of real-life situations and the repercussions of your actions in the world indicates a high level of professionalism and maturity.

10. Learn to identify the type of question and have a strategy for each.

It is impossible for you to predict the exact interview questions you may encounter, but if you learn to identify the different question *types* and common *themes* and have a strategy for each, you will have a better chance of acing them during your interview. We will identify these question types and go through strategies to answer them in the next chapter, so review them before and during practice!

11. Provide the most rational and common-sense solution that causes the least amount of harm to those involved.

Applicants often spend a considerable amount of time reading advanced medical ethics books, but that is not necessary and often leads to frustration. The interviewers know that you are not an ethicist, nor a practicing professional familiar with all the intricacies of your field. To show professionalism, all you need to do is demonstrate that you can make common sense decisions and come up with rational responses that cause as little harm to others as possible.

12. Get comfortable with awkward silences.

In timed interviews like the MMI, candidates often feel the need to keep talking until they run out of time or get cut off, instead of bringing their response to a firm conclusion. As a result, they compromise the quality of their answer for unnecessary quantity and end up displaying poor communication and time management skills! Remember, this is a test of your communication skills more than anything else. When you are being concise and your response is effective, you are likely to complete your answer before the time is up. If the interviewer does not have any follow-up questions, you need to be comfortable with the awkward silence that will ensue until the buzzer sounds.

13. Don't forget to say your goodbyes!

Remember when we talked about the primacy effect earlier? Your second-best friend during your interview is the *recency effect*. This is another well-documented principle in psychology, dictating that people remember the last piece of information presented to them in more detail than what was said earlier in a conversation. Therefore, it is critical that you give a positive impression before leaving your interview. It's not rocket science; simply smile, thank the interviewer for their time, and politely say goodbye before exiting the room.

14. Dedicate at least 6 to 8 weeks to prepare for the interview.

Think of your interview as a behavioral test. Just like for any other test, you must start preparing well in advance because it takes a long time to develop new habits and curb undesirable behaviors. In our experience, it takes at least 6 to 8 weeks to fully prepare for a medical school interview.

15. Familiarize yourself with professional ethics.

You will inevitably encounter interview questions that touch on professional ethics. For physicians, this includes topics like informed consent, patient autonomy, confidentiality, and professional boundaries, amongst others. Therefore, it would be beneficial for you to read some general books about professional ethics in the field of medicine. We don't have specific recommendations, but a Google or Amazon search should give you plenty of options, as can your university or college library.

16. Avoid overreliance on books and guides.

Books, like this one, are a good starting point for interview preparation, but once you have understood the background knowledge, it will be time to put theory into practice, which brings us to the next point.

17. Practice using realistic mock interviews.

Just like any other functional skill, the only way to improve your interview performance is to deliberately and repeatedly engage in the task. Reading interviews guides and sample questions is insufficient unless it is coupled with realistic practice. This can be achieved with simulations and mock interviews, which are effective in removing the 'fear of the unknown' and making you less nervous and more confident on the day of your interview.

18. Remember that PERFECT practice makes perfect.

Lastly, only *perfect* practice makes perfect. If you are practicing with ineffective strategies, you are going to form bad habits, which become difficult to correct and may impede your interview performance. Therefore, after you practice in simulations or mock interviews, it is crucial that you get feedback. This feedback should come from an *expert* such as a practicing health care professional, medical doctor, university professor, or anyone with a higher educational background, *not* a friend or family member. Only an expert will be able to give you a professional, objective assessment of your interview performance and recommendations on how to improve. This is the most effective way to prepare for your interview. Period.

When you enroll in one of BeMo's prep programs, you will get access to realistic mock interviews followed by one-on-one expert feedback from one of our admissions experts who goes over each of your responses, identifies your strengths and weaknesses, and tells you how to do better next time. We will continue to work with you until you are confident about your upcoming interview. To learn more, visit our website at www.BeMoMedInterview.com.

Now that you have seen the overview of the key strategies to acing your interview, let's dive into the different interview questions you might encounter and the specific strategies to use for each.

Are you ready? Let's begin!

CHAPTER VII

Proven Strategies to Prepare for and Ace Any Medical School Interview Question

While you cannot predict the exact questions you will be asked, you can certainly prepare for the *types* of questions you will encounter. That is why in this chapter, we break down the different types of questions for you and discuss the best strategies to approach each. Familiarizing yourself with these question types and associated strategies will ensure that, no matter what they ask you on the day of your interview, you will be able to give a well-organized, in-depth, and concise answer.

As we outline the different question types, you may be tempted to skip over a few, especially if you have heard that some question types were not used by a particular program in a previous cycle. Indeed, depending on the program and interview style they choose, you will be more likely to encounter some question types than others.

However, keep in mind that each school can change their interview format or the question types from one year to the next without any prior notice to applicants. This means that what you or your friend experienced the year before may not be what you encounter this year. Therefore, the best strategy is to make sure you are ready for every type of question, regardless of the historical trends for a specific school. The last thing you want on your interview day is to be bamboozled by questions you knew about but did not prepare for when you had the chance. Of course, it is also possible that you see a brand-new question type that is not discussed in this book. That is totally normal, and it is likely that the question type is newly developed. Rest assured that as long as you can answer 80% of the questions well, you are going to be in the 90th percentile out of all your peers, which is sufficient to help you become a successful applicant and a better individual. Our goal in this book is, thus, not to go over *all* possible types of questions, but rather to teach you those that are most common.

The 6 categories of question types we will look at in this chapter are:

- Personal Questions
- Program-Specific Questions
- MMI-Type Questions (Please note: Although these question types are common on MMIs, they can show up in *any* interview format. The other question types can also show up in MMIs.)
    a. Scenario- or situation-based
    b. Acting
    c. Picture-based
    d. Video-based
    e. Writing sample
- Policy-based or Hot Topics Questions
- Quirky Questions
- Collaborative or Task-Based Questions

For each question type, we will outline its characteristics and strategies for answering it.

1. Personal Questions

Personal questions are designed for the interviewer to get to know more about you and your unique life experiences. These types of questions, like interviews, can be characterized as *closed* (not based on any knowledge of your application) or *open* (based on at least some of the details in your application, including your grades, test scores, personal statement, or CV).

Personal questions are sometimes open-ended, for example, "Tell me about yourself." or "Why have you decided to pursue medicine?". They can also more specific, probing you about a positive or negative experience you have had or a personality trait. For example, you may be asked "What would you say is your greatest accomplishment?" or "Describe a time you had a conflict with a superior.". You may also be asked about the experiences on your application documents if you have an open interview. We briefly discuss the strategies to each of these types of personal questions below.

1. Open-ended personal questions

Open-ended personal questions tend to be the most challenging because you must give a genuine response that concisely threads together your motivations and multiple experiences. For these questions, remember not to regurgitate *every* experience you have ever had or try to mention every single item on your CV. Rather, be selective about the points you discuss so your answer can be concise. Focus on a maximum of 3 experiences you genuinely feel you learned a lot from and include detailed personal examples so you are showing, and not just telling, the interviewer what you learned. A good way to thread these experiences together is chronologically to ensure that your answer is easy to for the interviewer to follow. This will also make it easy for you to remember! Also be sure to link your experiences with good transitional phrases so that the interviewer can easily see the connections between them.

Crafting a concise but in-depth answer to an open-ended question is not easy. To prepare for these types of questions, you must sit down well in advance and spend time in introspection. What are three experiences that really highlight who you are as a person? What are the three biggest reasons you are pursuing medicine and not another profession? Avoid defaulting to clichés such as wanting to 'help people' because almost every profession allows you to help people in some way. Instead, take the time to reflect more deeply on your personal motivations so your answers are unique to you. Jot them down on a piece of paper and think through specific experiences and details you can use as supporting evidence. Also think about how each experience relates to the other, so that you can effectively transition between them. Once you have your main points and supporting details, and you know how they are all connected, you can begin practicing your answer out loud. Taking time to self-reflect will ensure you have an outline of your answer ready to go, and you will not feel flustered when answering these challenging questions.

2. *Questions about specific experiences or traits*

Now, let's turn to personal questions that ask about specific experiences or behavioral traits. Consider the question "Tell us about a time you resolved a conflict." as an example. The main mistake applicants make with this type of question is to spend all of their time describing an incidence when they resolved a conflict. The goal here is to not only recount the experience, but more importantly, to tell the interviewer what you *learned* from that experience and how you hope to *apply* those lessons to resolve future conflicts, especially situations you may encounter in the profession of medicine. Yes, you should highlight the lessons learned and skills developed even if the interviewer does not ask you to do so, because this is your chance to show your maturity and ability to self-reflect, learn, and change. To begin preparing for these questions, sit down with your application documents and ask yourself what you have learned from each of the experiences you have highlighted. What skills and values did you gain that will make you a better physician? Jot these down in point form on a piece of paper, then practice answering some example questions of this type.

You may have noticed that for any question you identify as *personal*, you must *always* provide a specific personal example that relates to the question. Here are three simple steps to help you structure each example:

Step #1: Describe the experience.

Most candidates think that this is the focus of the example they give. It's not! The description of the experience should be no more than 2 to 3 sentences. The purpose of describing a specific experience is to support the lessons you propose to have learned and the skills you claim to have demonstrated with tangible evidence. If you are describing a challenging situation or obstacle, be sure to include what you acted to overcome it and highlight the positive outcome.

While being concise with the description, it is also important to go in-depth and be specific. Compare the two examples below:

Vague example: While volunteering at the downtown hospital, I got the chance to meet many patients from different walks of life. Though we didn't always share the same culture, language, or education background, I was able to form meaningful relationships with them and make them feel at ease while they waited for their doctors.

Specific example: While volunteering at the downtown hospital, I got the chance to meet many patients from different walks of life. One of these was a woman named Sabrina who immigrated to the U.S. from the Philippines. Though she didn't speak English and I didn't speak Tagalog, I was able to relay the nurse's messages to her using a series of hand gestures and I continued to sit with her in the waiting room to make her feel at ease in the unfamiliar hospital environment.

Note that the first example and the second example are demonstrating the same interpersonal skills. However, the second is much more tangible to the interviewer because the candidate discusses a specific interaction they had with a patient rather than speaking to their experience as a whole.

Step #2: Identify the lessons learned and/or skills exhibited

This should be the focus of your example. Interviewers are most interested in knowing what lessons and skills you learned from you past that are transferable to your future. This helps them assess your potential and suitability for the profession. If you are discussing an observation you made, say what traits you saw in the professionals you worked with that you admire and want to emulate. If you were directly involved in the interaction you described, then explicitly outline the traits you exhibited. It may be helpful when giving an example to work backwards and identify the traits you want to discuss first, then come up with the specific experience that would best illustrate these traits. Be sure to familiarize yourself with the skills and competencies that medical schools are after in their candidates. You can do this by researching the mission and candidate selection criteria for each school you are interviewing at. For a broader overview, see the competencies lists published by the institutions governing medical schools in your region, such as the core competencies list published by the AAMC.

Step #3: Relate those lessons and skills to your future profession.

Lastly, you can connect your skills to your future work environment to demonstrate to the interviewers that you understand how your skills can help you succeed in your future role. It is always more convincing if you can identify the specific context in which the skills or traits will become useful. Compare the following:

> *Weak application:* I hope to continue to use my strong communication skills and cultural competency to connect with patients in the future.

Strong application: As someone who aspires to work with underrepresented groups in the downtown area, I know I will encounter many patients who do not share my cultural, linguistic, and educational background. However, I strongly believe that I will be able to overcome these barriers with my excellent communication skills and cultural competency to form meaningful, lasting relationships with those I serve.

In the first application, the candidate states that their skills will be helpful in their future career but remains vague about how and when they might be used. In the second application, the candidate makes a much stronger connection between their skills and their future profession, identifying the specific patient population their skills will benefit.

2. Program-Specific Questions

When you are interviewing for medical school, you are interviewing to attend a particular program. Therefore, you may be asked questions about that school or program. Every medical school has a mission statement and values they espouse, as well as particular qualities they are looking for in their student body, so the interviewer will want to ensure you are a good fit for their program.

Examples of program-specific questions are "Why would you like to attend our school?", "One of our core values is patient-centered care. How have you exemplified this?", and "If you could change anything about our program, what would it be?".

To answer these types of questions well, you will need to get familiar with the school or program, their mission statement, values, curriculum, research opportunities, and extracurricular activities or clubs available to medical students. Hopefully you already did a lot of this research when you decided to apply there, but here are some questions to get you thinking as you prepare: Where is the school located and what are the demographics of the population in that area? What is the profile of the current medical school class? Do a lot of the students have shadowing, volunteering, and/or research experience? Does the school especially want students to pursue primary care, or careers in academia or administration? You can find this information by visiting the school website. If the school allows you to visit, you can even talk to someone in their admissions office or a current student and ask questions about the program, the curriculum, and the current student body.

Once you have thoroughly done your research about the program, sit down and identify 3 unique reasons why you would like to attend that particular program and which of your experiences make you a good fit. These can be reasons relating to aspects of the curriculum, how you reflect the school's core values, how you fit into the student body, or even what you like about the location of the school. Remember to always use your experiences as examples and discuss what you learned. If patient-centered care is valued by the school, you can talk about the skills you have garnered through your volunteering or shadowing experiences. If they value research, discuss your most interesting research project and why you are committed to this area of study. If you are asked what improvements or modifications you would make to the program, identify the area that needs change and use the opportunity to say how you will *personally* make this happen. This demonstrates to the interviewer that you are proactive and willing take responsibility. For example, if the school does not have a student wellness program and you have volunteering experience in mental health, you may want to propose starting a program that promotes work-life balance and brings mental health resources to the student body at that school.

Reflect on these points now so you are not coming up with them during your interview. Your answer to "Why our program?" is a way to show the interviewer that you are interested in their program and set on attending their school, which can in turn increase your chances of admission.

3. MMI Questions

a. Scenario- or situation-based

In scenario questions, you will be given a hypothetical role in a hypothetical situation and asked how you would approach or solve it.

These types of questions are common even in traditional interviews, so the strategies you will learn have a broad application.

The question prompts are based on real-life situations and may not be related to the profession of medicine. For example, you might be asked how you would resolve a conflict between two friends, or how you would deal with a disgruntled customer in a coffee shop. As you can imagine, a scenario question can touch upon many different themes. We discuss 23 of these below.

23 Scenario Themes

1. *Conflict of interest*

A conflict of interest refers to any scenario in which individuals, contrary to their obligations and absolute duties to act for the benefit of those they serve, exploit their relationships or status for their own personal benefit. For example, a hospital director is in a conflict of interest if she insists on using products from a company that periodically sends her gifts. A teacher who is grading tests of his close friend's son is also in a conflict of interest.

Here are a few really interesting examples for you to think about. A university professor in charge of education research who creates a for-profit admission screening company from his publicly-funded research is said to be in a conflict of interest because he would not be able to objectively judge new advances in the field if such advances threaten the existence of his newly formed for-profit venture. A university professor who is a director of a for-profit company, such as an admissions screening company, is in a conflict of interest if she speaks publicly – for example, at an information webinar for students taking the admissions test – and introduces herself as a professor of the university instead of one of the directors of the company. Similarly, a public university that is tasked with advancing knowledge is in a conflict of interest when its ability to advance discovery is impeded by its interests in a for-profit spin-off company. Do any of these sound familiar?

2. Ethical or moral dilemma

These are scenarios in which any decision you make will lead to the violation of some moral or ethical code. For example, let's say you are a physician in an emergency room and you simultaneously receive two patients who both need a kidney transplant to survive, but you only have one kidney available. Choosing either of the patients would harm the other. Or, you witness your best friend stealing from her abusive boss at work who has not paid your friend for the past 2 months. Reporting the unethical behavior of the boss would help your friend, but she will likely also face legal consequences for stealing. The interviewer will want to see that you can make ethically and morally sound decisions even when scenarios appear to be impossible.

3. Professional boundaries, obligations, and ethics

These types of scenarios deal with instances in which effective and appropriate interactions and relationships between the professionals and the public are violated. For instance, a professor having relations with his student outside of the academic setting would be overstepping his professional boundaries with that student.

4. Scope of practice

All professionals have a certain scope of practice. These are laws and regulations that define the procedures, actions, and processes that are permitted for a licensed professional. For example, only medical doctors can prescribe medication within their scope of practice. If any other professional prescribes medication, they are said to be acting outside of their scope of practice. Similarly, a physician who has specialized in the neurology cannot advise patients on the pathologies of the kidney; they would be acting outside of their scope. Likewise, a math teacher is best suited to teach math and not genetics. We can extend this notion to the general boundaries of responsibility for non-professionals as well. For example, as a friend of a patient, you would be overstepping your boundaries by inquiring of the patient's condition from their physician. As a volunteer at a homeless shelter, you would be acting outside of your role by suggesting treatment options to those who are visiting the shelter. Though these may seem like obvious boundaries to observe, candidates often suggest solutions or courses of action that overstep them in their responses.

5. *Social and current events awareness*

Some scenario questions incorporate real policy issues to test your awareness of current events and news about the profession. These are questions that ask you to address an issue (e.g. indigenous health) in a specific role (e.g. as a member of the indigenous community, a health care professional, or a policy maker). These types of questions demand you to navigate the situation as if it were a scenario-type question while incorporating what you know about the real issue. It is therefore a good idea for you to be aware of all the news and challenges faced by your future profession, which you would do anyways to prepare for policy or hot topic question. (See the discussion on these questions for how to stay up-to-date on current issues.)

6. *Autonomy support*

Autonomy support refers to the right of individuals to make decisions about their own well-being. This is referred to as *patient autonomy* in medicine. The health care provider is not allowed to make treatment decisions for the patient as this would violate patient autonomy. Rather, it is the responsibility of physicians to educate and inform the patient using the latest scientific evidence so that the patient can make the most informed decision on their own. An example outside the field of medicine is when lawyers provide expert solutions to their clients. Lawyers can only present possible solutions and their outcomes based on their expertise but cannot make a decision on behalf of their client. The same concept is equally important in other professions and in all circumstances in which the professional's job is to educate those under their care based on their expertise in the field so that care receivers can make sound decisions autonomously.

People's autonomy to think, decide, and act must be respected. As a future professional you must apply this mindset in your daily life and in scenario questions where you are given the role of an expert.

There are only extreme cases when professionals can violate this rule, such as when an individual is not of sound mind or physically incapacitated to an extent that makes them unable to communicate and make decisions. In other extreme cases, such as when someone is likely to cause harm to themselves or others, the ethical obligation to support autonomy is replaced by the ethical and, in some cases, legal obligation to intervene and protect the health and safety of the individuals involved. There are always exceptions to the principles discussed and you must develop the maturity of thought to exercise good judgment and flexibility when faced with extreme cases.

7. *Informed consent*

Another concept related to autonomy support is informed consent. Once you have provided the best possible solutions to those under your care, you are responsible for answering any and all of their questions regarding the solutions and potential consequences to make sure they fully understand their options and can make an informed decision. Once care receivers are fully informed, they can give informed consent to either receive or refuse a specific course of action. For example, as a nurse, you must address all questions about a treatment option, or request the help of a doctor to do so when the questions are outside of your scope of practice, so that the patient is truly able to give informed consent to that treatment. An excellent exercise for you to do right now is to think of at least 5 different professions and come up with examples of how autonomy support and informed consent are integral parts of these professions. Then, apply this to 5 everyday scenarios that involve an expert and a novice or a supervisor and a subordinate.

8. Evidence-based practice

Practicing professionals are expected to make decisions and provide care and expertise based on scientific evidence, rather than gut feeling or personal opinions. In the absence of scientific evidence, the best source of information is experience accumulated in the profession, such as from case studies. Therefore, whether you are a medical doctor, a teacher, a dentist, or a speech therapist, your decisions must be based on sound evidence.

This does not mean that you need to have all the scientific knowledge to do well on a scenario question! Recall that interviewers are not trying to test your background knowledge in a particular profession because you will be learning much of this in medical school after you are accepted. Rather, they want to see that you can identify the missing evidence and discuss how different pieces of evidence would influence your next steps. Therefore, you must incorporate evidence-based practice into your fact-gathering procedure in complex scenarios with many unknowns and show that you are capable of making decisions based on evidence. We will discuss how to structure this portion of your answer when we discuss the strategies to approaching all scenario questions below.

9. Rural vs. city practice

Scenarios set in a rural context require you to address specific concerns. You must have a good understanding of what the challenges are for professionals working in a rural setting and for community members trying to access care, what the advantages and disadvantages are for both parties, whether the care provider or the care receiver comes first when considering these pros and cons, who should decide where someone ought to practice, and so forth. Knowing the answers to these questions will enable you to navigate scenarios that play on this theme with confidence.

10. Legal awareness

This type of question requires you to have common sense awareness of what procedures or actions are legal vs. illegal. In general, the decisions you make must be legally sound in almost all circumstances. We say "almost all" because there may be cases where doing what is legal might cause more harm to those involved. These scenarios are rare, but they are challenging for the unprepared candidate and those lacking maturity of thought because they present a seemingly impossible ethical dilemma. For these situations in particular, it is crucial to identify the most vulnerable party and support the decisions you make by prioritizing their well-being and the well-being of others who are directly or indirectly involved.

Keep in mind there will also be times when a legal policy brought up in your scenario is outdated and should be systematically reformed. This is why, in countries using the common-law system, the decision-making process in unusual cases can be influenced by a body of unwritten laws based on legal precedents established by the courts. This body of unwritten laws can sometimes become the basis for new legislation to be proposed and enacted. The common-law system is practiced by almost one third of all countries around the world, including the U.S., the U.K., Canada, Australia, and New Zealand. Laws are continuously modified to keep up with the changes in our social environment and advances in technology, science, and general human understanding.

As a disclaimer, note that we are not lawyers and we cannot provide any legal advice because it is outside of our scope of practice. If you want to learn more, you must contact a lawyer. However, remember that your interview is no more a test of your legal knowledge as it is a test of your medical knowledge. Rather, interviewers want to see that you have the maturity to react based on common sense.

11. Alternative solutions

In almost all professions, there are alternatives to generally accepted practices. For example, in medicine, alternative solutions include those provided by homeopathic medicine, naturopathic medicine, and chiropractic medicine. In teaching, alternative to traditional schooling include homeschooling or boarding schools. You may encounter scenarios that require you to show awareness of alternative solutions and professions and know when and how, if at all, you might recommend such a solution.

12. Non-judgmental approach

Now, this is a special theme because all scenario-based questions fall under this category in some way. As you may recall, we talked about how you need to approach all interview questions using a non-biased approach so that you do not jump to conclusions or take extreme positions. However, some scenario stations will specifically frame an issue in a way that would lead unprepared candidates to make a snap judgment about the situation or the character of an individual involved. For example, you may get a scenario in which a student coming in to seek help from a professor is described as always being late to class and rarely submitting work on-time. Though this might suggest that the student is irresponsible and does poorly in class, you cannot make those assumptions based on the intentionally misleading information. The student could be extremely bright and hard-working but facing personal difficulties that are not revealed in the prompt. Being non-judgmental at all times requires you to be on the lookout for biasing facts in the questions you encounter.

As a quick exercise, think about the last 2 important decisions you had to make quickly about a situation or a person. Did you gather all the facts first or did you jump to a conclusion right away? How was your action influenced by your initial judgment or assumptions?

13. Conflict resolution

This type of scenario, as the name implies, deals with situations that require you to intervene to resolve a conflict. This can be an internal conflict, a conflict between two individuals unknown to you, or a conflict between you and a superior, a peer, or a colleague. The scenarios will vary in detail, but the essence remains the same. You have to show that you are able to maturely and professionally resolve any conflict and come up with an agreeable solution for all parties involved.

14. Global issues related to the profession

There may be scenarios that assess your awareness of global issues that might impact your future profession. Once again, the only way to show such knowledge is to continuously read articles, scientific papers, and reports related to your profession from international governing bodies and other reliable sources. After all, if you are truly interested in your future profession, wouldn't it make sense for you to obsess over everything there is to know about it?

15. Cultural sensitivity

As a future professional you are going to encounter people from different cultural, social, racial, and religious backgrounds. Often, such differences lead to different behaviors, expectations, and beliefs and your job is to show your understanding without any judgment while providing the best care or service possible. For example, what would you do if you were a teacher and a student objected to an exam date due to a religious holiday? Would you accommodate the student or would you remain strict about the exam date? If you do decide to accommodate them, how would you do so while being fair to other students?

16. Empathy

Being sensitive to others' emotions and having the capacity to understand and experience the feelings of others is a critical skill in any profession. When you understand those you serve, you are better able to react and attend to their inquiries, needs, and fears. Importantly, when you are truly empathetic, you can foster a trusting relationship, which in turn promotes better care delivery because those under your care will be more likely to listen to and implement your recommendations.

17. Confidentiality

As a professional you have a moral and even legal obligation to keep all information about those under your care confidential at all time. This means you must not reveal the details of any of your conversations or findings about your care receivers to anyone who is not directly involved in providing care for them, including your own close friends and family members. You have to truly understand and display a genuine appreciation that care receivers are revealing very sensitive and sometimes embarrassing information to you as a professional. Therefore, maintaining confidentiality is critical to maintaining trusting relationships with your future patients. Furthermore, it is important to apply the same principles even in your personal life. If your family members, friends, or peers share confidential information with you, you should appreciate them opening up to you, and importantly, not share that information with others.

18. Beneficence ('do good')

Beneficence requires that you act with the intent of doing good for the care receiver involved. This goes hand-in-hand with the next theme.

19. Nonmaleficence ('do no harm')

Nonmaleficence requires that you act without the intention to harm the care receiver involved or others in society. There are different opinions about the concept of harm or doing bad. In health care professions, a harmful action is one that worsens the condition of the patient. In some cases, it is difficult for health care providers to successfully apply the *do no harm* principle if the action required to achieve it runs counter to their morals and beliefs. Refusing to act in cases like this is called conscientious objection. We will discuss it shortly.

20. Justice

The term *justice* means fairness in treatment. It opposite, *injustice*, therefore occurs when similar cases do not receive similar treatment. To make just decisions in the context of health care, these four main factors must be evaluated:

i. fair distribution of scarce resources,

ii. competing needs,

iii. rights and obligations, and

iv. potential conflicts with established legislation.

21. Patient-centered care

In a nutshell, being a patient-centered healthcare provider means putting the patients' needs before your own. In the introduction to their article *Ethics, risk, and patient-centered care: How collaboration between clinical ethicists and risk management leads to respectful patient care*, Sine and Sharpe clearly state, "Patient-centered care is driven in part by the ethical principle of autonomy and considers patients' cultural traditions, personal preferences, values, family situations, and lifestyles." The authors continue to explain that when healthcare providers do not meet patient needs or understand their expectations, the patient may be dissatisfied with their healthcare services. An additional article by Linda Bell entitled, *Patient-Centered Care* stated, "the goal of patient-centered care is to see the patient and family as a single unit. That is, care for the patient includes the family, and decisions made about patient care include the patient's and family's wishes."

22. Conscientious objection

This is a sincere objection to participate in an act by reason of moral and ethical beliefs that influence one's views on life. Conscientious objection in medicine is highly relevant to cases involving physician-assisted dying and abortion. A health care provider's moral and ethical conflict and disagreement about an act, such as physician-assisted dying or abortion, may prevent them from engaging in such act, although it may be legal in their country, state, or province. In the case where conscientious objection comes into play, it becomes important to respect the physician's autonomy. However, they may still recommend other physicians who would not be in the same conflict, or the patient may need to seek out other physicians who do not have conscientious objections to providing the treatment or procedures they need.

23. Communication

Communication is not only an important skill that you need to demonstrate throughout your interview, it is also a theme in all scenario questions. In any situational question, interviewers are assessing how you gather information from other parties involved in the scenario, how you propose to relay your ideas to them, how you address their needs, how you get them to cooperate with you on your solutions and so forth. Therefore, you must not only communicate your points clearly, you must also demonstrate that you are able to communicate effectively in hypothetical situations to audiences of different backgrounds.

Most scenario-type questions incorporate multiple themes simultaneously. For example, in a situation involving a patient and physician, themes such as patient-centered care, autonomy support, confidentiality, cultural sensitivity, and so forth can all be at play. The type of situation you encounter will determine how you should to navigate it, including what you say to the other parties involved, how you relay that information, and what the best solutions are. Therefore, before you respond to a scenario question, you should always identify the themes as this will help you to formulate an appropriate plan of action. The best way to understand these concepts is to see them in action in sample questions. Therefore, pay attention to the scenario questions in *Chapter XII: 20 Sample Medical School Interview Questions with Expert Responses and Analyses* and see if you can identify the themes present in each. You will be able to continue practicing this for the scenario questions in *Chapter XIII: 100 Practice Medical School Interview Questions.*

Steps to Answering Any Scenario Question

Given the potentially overwhelming number of theme combinations, scenario- or situation-based questions tend to cause a lot of anxiety for interviewees. However, there is one straightforward structure to use when approaching *any* such question. Knowing it by heart will help you build confidence and competence as you practice. The following steps may sound familiar because they were briefly discussed in *Chapter VI: Pre-Mortem: 18 Proven Strategies to Prepare for and Ace Any Medical School Interview*. However, since they are especially important for scenario-based questions, we reiterate them here and encourage you to familiarize yourself with them as quickly as possible.

Step 1: Identify the most pressing issue.

Do not rush a scenario question. Take a step back and identify what the most pressing issue is first to make clear to the interviewer exactly what the focus of your answer is. Whenever you read a scenario, ask yourself "Who are the vulnerable parties?". Their safety and well-being should be your top priority and ensuring their well-being is the pressing issue you are focusing on. You only have a few minutes to deliver your response, so if you miss this step, you may give a response that is irrelevant or even propose a solution that is dangerous and irresponsible.

If you are having trouble identifying the most pressing issue, think about the consequences of doing absolutely *nothing*. For example, what would happen if someone is inebriated and you let them drive? What would happen if you get into a conflict with someone and you do absolutely nothing to resolve it? What would happen if one of your team members refuses to do their part and you do nothing to address that problem? Often, doing this exercise will help you to identify the individual or group that would be most impacted by your action or inaction.

Step 2: Reserve judgment until you have all the facts.

Next, you have to gather all of the facts prior to formulating a plan of action. Most scenario questions are missing a lot of crucial information. This is done intentionally to see whether you are going to assume certain facts that are not explicitly available. If you are judgmental and make assumptions, your response will lack nuance and you will be viewed as lacking maturity. Mature professionals, like physicians, consider multiple perspectives at once and reserve judgment until they have a complete picture of the situation.

Consider a situation in which you are working in a group setting and one of the group members complains to you that another member is not contributing enough to the project. A lot of information is missing from this prompt. What has each member already contributed? What is considered an adequate contribution? Does each group member have a clear idea of what is expected of them? Is this a one-time occurrence? Is the group member ill or dealing with other extenuating circumstances? Are the two members on good terms with each other, or is there a history of animosity between them? If you jump to a conclusion and say something like, "Well, in this case I have no choice but to report the slacking group member to our professor," then you have already lost all the points for that station because you acted on assumptions without gathering the facts first.

To approach the situation non-judgmentally, you need to explicitly show the interviewers your thought pattern by verbalizing how you would fill in the information gaps. After you have identified the pressing issue for the group work scenario, you might say, "First, without making a hasty decision, I would have a *private*, non-judgmental conversation with the two team members to gather more information. During these conversations, I would ask each group member to articulate their understanding of the work expected of them, and whether they feel adequately supported in completing that work. I would also want to ask each of them for their sense of how the group is getting along, and whether they, or anyone else in the group, are experiencing extenuating circumstances that may impede progress on their part of the work." First, note the emphasis on the word "private". Asking someone sensitive questions in public could embarrass them, so demonstrate your emotional and social intelligence by explicitly saying that the conversation will be private – and make this a habit in your own life as well. The only exception to this rule is when you have to deal with an emergency, and you do not have the time for a private conversation. Next, verbalize the kinds of questions you might ask during your private conversation in the scenario. By posing the right questions in a hypothetical situation, you will demonstrate your information-gathering skills while also highlighting your maturity when navigating complex and sensitive situations.

Step 3: Determine who is directly and indirectly involved.

As part of your fact-gathering and investigation process, you must, of course, identify all the parties that are directly and indirectly involved in the scenario.

For example, imagine a scenario where you are the physician who needs to communicate a piece of information to a patient. Although in the scenario there are only 2 individuals directly involved (you and the patient), the information can, at times, also indirectly affect the patient's family and/or co-workers, your fellow physicians and colleagues, and/or the medical profession at large. For instance, if the news is about the diagnosis of a serious illness, the family and close friends may need to be involved in caring for the patient, and the patient may no longer be able to work, therefore affecting their co-workers. Depending on the illness, the treatment may require a whole team of medical professionals. If, say, it is a unique case, then even researchers from other institutions may get involved.

Mature professionals can identify those who will be directly and indirectly impacted by their decisions. Conversely, those who do not have maturity of thought will only identify those who are directly involved and fail to see the larger ramifications of their decisions and actions.

Step 4: Choose the best solution(s) based on moral, ethical, legal, and scientific reasoning.

Once you have considered a few practical options, choose the most rational solution. This is the one that causes the least harm to those directly and indirectly involved in the scenario, adheres to existing laws and policies, respects professional boundaries, and so forth. You will also need to *explain* the reasoning behind your thoughts and proposed actions. If you have to entertain multiple hypothetical situations and different solutions to each of them, we recommend using the 'if, then' structure. For example, "*If*, I am convinced that my friend is intoxicated, but is only going to their car to grab their phone and call a taxi, *then* I would not interfere and even offer to help them call a ride. On the other hand, *if* I am convinced that they are going to drive away intoxicated, *then...*"

Note that you need to be thinking about all of these elements (what the pressing issue is, what information is missing, who is directly and indirectly involved, and what the best solution is) *while* you read or hear the question from the interviewer. This may seem very difficult, if not impossible, to do within such time constraints, yet these thinking patterns can absolutely be learned, refined, and facilitated over time. This is precisely why perfect practice is so important. As you initially start practicing, follow the step-by-step strategy slowly and methodically in order to solidify the process. Once you are comfortable with it, this process will become faster and automatic.

Before moving on to the next MMI question type, we would like to share with you ***three master strategies from our CEO*** that will help you ace scenario-type questions:

1. Start applying these to situations in your daily life. Begin to identify the moral, ethical, legal issues and so forth in the interactions you engage in or observe on your ride home from school, in the grocery store, in the classroom, on the news, on your favorite show, even in the conversation you had with your mother this morning. For the situations you are personally involved in, follow the steps above to resolve them! That is, identify the pressing issue, remain non-judgmental and gather information, and determine all the parties involved *before* acting. For situations you observe, go through the though exercise of what you would do in the shoes of each person directly involved.
2. Take it a step further and create scenario and follow-up questions from the situations that arise in your daily life as if you were the test administrator! One way to become an expert in answering scenario questions is to create questions daily. Do this simple exercise for 15 minutes a day for the next 30 days and we guarantee you will notice a significant improvement.
3. Teach these life-changing strategies to your family and friends. You know you have truly mastered a skill when you are able to teach the material to someone else.

These strategies will not only help you ace scenario-type questions, but they will help you become a mature professional and a better person, which is the primary goal of this book.

b. Acting

Another question type that can come up in MMIs is acting or role-playing. At these stations, you are given a prompt that describes a certain situation and your role in it. You are then asked to enter the room and act as if the situation is actually happening, usually by interacting with an actor or another candidate. For example, the prompt could be "Your friend, John, who you've known for 10 years, has invited you to his place to discuss a personal matter with you. Walk in and begin talking to your friend, John." When you enter the room, you would act as if you had just arrived at your friend's house and respond to your acting partner accordingly. Other acting situations you may encounter include delivering bad news to a patient, resolving a conflict or de-escalating a situation, and so forth.

Whatever the situation, you will need to understand your role and your relationship with the others involved and tune into the emotions of those people. Remember to always acknowledge the way the other person is feeling and to take time to listen and empathize with them. After they have had a chance to express their emotions, provide reassurance, and only then begin to offer solutions. Sometimes the actors may be instructed to be highly uncooperative and to continuously attempt to escalate the situation. Your job is to remain composed and to resolve the situation professionally, even if the actor is insufferable, annoying, or impolite. Remember, physicians deal with challenging patients and stressed colleagues regularly and they must always remain calm and collected.

In all acting stations, there are two very important things to remember. First, make sure that the words, tone, and body language you use are appropriate for the situation. For example, if a friend shares a piece of good news, it is completely appropriate to smile and tell her how happy you are for her. In contrast, smiling would be inappropriate during an acting station where your friend told you she just lost a loved one. Secondly, always put yourself in the other person's shoes and verbalize the empathy you have for them. For example, if you have to give someone bad news, it is a good idea to say something like, "I know how difficult this must be for you, and it may seem overwhelming. I will be here to help you through this." Acting does not come naturally to most people, and these stations may feel very uncomfortable at first. To prepare for acting stations, pay attention to the acting next time you watch a particularly emotional scene on television or in a movie, practice delivering both good and bad news in a mirror, ask a friend to roleplay with you, or sign up for one of BeMo's interview preparation programs. With thoughtful preparation, you can enter acting stations calmly and successfully navigate any type of situation.

c. Picture-based

In picture-based stations, you will be presented with a photo or an abstract picture representing a social challenge facing our world today and asked to share your thoughts. For example, you may be shown a picture of a mother caring for her child in a war-stricken country or in a time of famine. Respond to such questions by describing who or what is in the image, for example people's clothing and facial expressions, the weather, or the dwellings or buildings. Your next step is to succinctly share about how the image makes your feel, and/or explain your understanding of the social situation. When appropriate, you can also demonstrate your empathy and offer solutions. While these types of questions are rare, you should still prepare for them in case they turn up.

You must have some understanding of world issues and hot topics to do well on this type of question. We will discuss how to stay up-to-date on these issues in the section on policy-type questions.

d. Video-based

Video-based questions are also quite rare. In these types of questions, you will watch a short video about a hypothetical situation (much like the scenarios we discussed above) and be asked to explain how you would react. Alternatively, you may see a discussion about a policy and then be asked about your opinion. Whatever the content of the video is, use the strategy for that question type, whether it be scenario or policy.

e. Writing sample

While it is most common be asked to deliver your answers verbally, you may sometimes be asked to write or type your response. Writing stations are used for three primary reasons: 1) to obtain a writing sample from each candidate, 2) to increase the number of independent scores per candidate without increasing the number of interviewers, and 3) to increase the number of candidates interviewed without increasing the number of interviewers. This writing sample gives the admissions committee another chance to assess your written communication, a very important skill for a physician. Unlike your personal statement, which you had a long time to prepare and submit, you have a limited amount of time to write your response during an interview, and you certainly will not have a second person to help you revise it. Including an additional writing station also means that each candidate receives one more score and more candidates can be interviewed with no additional cost to the university.

Your approach to these types of stations should be no different from the strategies we have discussed for the various question types. Start by carefully considering the question, your main points, and the organization of your response. Careful planning is important because disorganization in a written essay is much more noticeable than in a verbal response. In addition, remember to leave yourself a bit of time at the end to re-read and edit your response. Be sure to check the essay for completeness and fix any grammar or spelling errors. The program may claim that grammar and spelling will not affect your score, but a polished written response is always preferable to a sloppy one.

4. Policy-Based or Hot Topics Questions

Policy-based or hot topics questions will ask for your thoughts on a newly proposed or controversial policy. Any time you are asked about your views or opinions, there are certain steps you should take to formulate a positive and unbiased answer. Avoid stating your opinion on an issue without first considering all sides of the argument. The best way to approach policy type questions is as follows:

Step 1: Show your awareness of the policy, topic, or issue

Start with a general statement that shows your awareness of the policy, the complexities surrounding the issue, and why such a policy may be proposed in the first place. This shows the interviewer you have a good grasp of the topic being discussed and that you are aware there are multiple sides to the issue. Additionally, referring to any recent news regarding the issue demonstrates your knowledge of current events. To do this effectively, you need to have a good grounding in the current hot topics in the profession of medicine, both locally and globally. Set time aside *each week* to browse local and national news websites, as well as your state or provincial medical association websites to ensure that your knowledge is up-to-date. You do not need to be an expert on any of these topics, but you do need to have general awareness and understanding of the key points and arguments.

Step 2: Discuss the PROs and CONs

Once you have introduced your answer and spoken generally about the complexities around the policy at hand, begin examining the specific benefits and drawbacks that need to be considered prior to taking a stance on the issue. At this point, you will outline pros and cons from the point of view of those affected by the policy. Present the positives and negatives from the patient, student, or client's point of view before the positives and negatives for the physician or other professionals. This shows that you consider the well-being of those under your care first before considering what is best for you.

Step 3: Take a stance and provide clear solutions

Based on the evidence that you have presented, you will then discuss where you stand on the issue. A common misconception is that the most important part of your response to a policy question is the ultimate decision you make; this is not the case! Instead, what matters most is your ability to articulate your thought process when analyzing a complex issue. When committing to a final stance on a policy issue, it is a good rule of thumb to side with the option that does the most good and the least harm for the most vulnerable parties involved. Alternatively, you can provide a unique solution or compromise that would benefit all parties. Keep in mind that if you take this approach, the interviewer may press you to make a decision. If this happens, be prepared to choose one option over another while providing an explanation for your decision. Again, if you have already discussed the complexities of the policy issue and can articulate why you are making that choice, you will do well on this type of question, regardless of the final decision you make.

In general, when it comes to policy-type questions, avoid starting with your own position on the policy, taking an extreme point of view, providing one-sided answers, or allowing your emotions to guide your response. Take a step back and consider the pros and cons for all individuals affected by the policy. Remember, the way you approach the question and discuss your thought process is far more important than your ultimate decision. These issues are controversial for a reason; there are strong arguments to be made for both sides!

To help you prepare, we will provide a list of some major points of debate in medicine in the next chapter. Familiarize yourself with these topics so that you are able to present thorough, unbiased answers if you encounter them in your interview.

5. Quirky Questions

Sometimes, you get asked a question that just seems, well, weird! Have you ever been asked which organ of the body you would be? Or what superpower you would like to have? How about being asked to teach the interviewer how to do something in a few minutes? These quirky questions are designed to surprise you and throw you off your game.

One of the main reasons these types of questions are asked is to see how you react under stress!

Of course, now that you know you can get asked these types of questions, you can develop a strategy and answer them calmly. Take a step back and plan for a few seconds before beginning your answer. It is always better to gather your thoughts and execute a well-organized response than to give an unplanned, rambling answer. Interestingly for these types of questions, interviewers care little about the direct answer to the question. Do the interviewers really want to know which organ you wish to be or what superpower you wish to have? No! What they are truly after is an explanation of *why* you are choosing that particular organ or superpower. You can strategically use your answer as a platform to discuss an aspect of your personality you wish for them to know. Do not just say you want to be a liver because livers are cool. Instead, say you would be the liver because the liver is resilient, like yourself. You can then provide some personal examples as evidence of your resilience, just as we discussed for personal questions above. Do not just say that you wish to go back in time because time-travel is awesome. Rather, say you wish you could go back in time to see and learn from your beloved grandmother who passed away a few years ago. As you can see, a strong answer to a quirky question should do more than just answer the question; it should also showcase one or more of your important traits.

What about if you are asked to teach the interviewer something in a few minutes? A lot of candidates panic at questions like this because they are unsure what kind of skill to teach in such a short amount of time. Again, it is not *what* you teach but *how* you do so that is important. Choose a hobby of yours, like a sport or fine art, or a language other than English, and teach the interviewer the basics of that skill. If you play tennis, for example, teach the interviewer the proper stance for hitting a forehand. Keeping in mind that what you are truly demonstrating here is your communication and collaboration skills, so break the task down into 3 to 4 easy-to-follow steps and check in with the interviewer throughout the teaching process to see if they have any questions or need clarification.

Take some time to think about how you would answer the example questions above to prepare for these types of quirky questions on interview day.

6. Collaborative or Task-Based Questions

Collaborative questions can take on many forms. You may be asked to work with another candidate or the interviewer to solve a problem, create a plan, teach each other something, argue opposing sides of an issue, act out a scenario, and so forth. In medicine, you will be working other members of a team, each with their own expertise and responsibilities. You will also work collaboratively with patients to ensure their health and well-being. Therefore, you must be able to work effectively with a wide range of personalities to succeed in this profession.

The key to acing such a question is remembering to *collaborate* with the other candidate or candidates so that you *all* succeed, rather than trying to outshine them. While it may feel as though you are being directly compared with the other interviewee(s), it is common for an entire group to perform very well or very poorly. The best candidates are inclusive, encouraging other interviewees to express their opinions. So, make sure you are not fixated on getting your opinion out there. Listen, engage with others, and solicit feedback!

A subset of collaborative questions are task-based questions. These typically involve a drawing or building task. At this kind of station, you will be asked to describe an image or object to another interviewee or the interviewer. The other person will then have to reproduce the image or object without having seen it. Alternatively, you may have to reproduce the image or object another candidate is describing. The drawing or building question is used to assess whether you approach problems in an organized and logical manner, whether you possess strong communication skills, whether you can patiently guide a naive participant through a complex task using accessible language, and so forth. Remember, you will be explaining complex concepts to patients and colleagues in your future career. The interviewer wants to see that you have the ability do so.

The following is an example of images on a sheet of paper you may be asked to describe at a drawing station.

Before you begin, take a step back and orient the other person. Make sure they are prepared with a pen and paper and understand the task at hand. Next, give a general overview of the picture or object they are about to draw. For example, you might say, "Orient the sheet of paper vertically. On it, there is are four equally spaced, black-and-white figures arranged in a two-by-two array. The array takes up the top half of the page, and each figure measures about 4 inches by 4 inches." Only after you have properly oriented the other person should you ask them to begin drawing. After each step, make sure to pause and ask the other applicant or interviewer if they are following you or if they have any questions. This is very important. You do not want to spend five minutes describing an image in detail only to find that you lost your drawer after your first instruction! Soliciting feedback from the other person will make you stand out as a candidate who listens and adjusts their strategy to help others achieve a goal.

If you are given a simple line drawing or geometric object, we recommend that you use the Cartesian system of x- and y-coordinates to describe the image to the drawer. To do this, ask them to draw the x- and y-axes along the bottom and left side of the page so that the origin of the graph, (x0, y0), is at the bottom left corner. Then, ask the person to label equally spaced points on both the x- and y-axes from 1 to 9. That way, you know that your scales will be the same, so that the point (x5, y5) will correspond to the exact middle of the page both for you and for the drawer.

Once you have oriented the drawer, you will look at your image and decide how many points it must be divided into. For example, if you had to describe a 1 inch by 1 inch square at the bottom left corner of the page, you would tell the drawer that the image you would like them to reproduce is made up of four points, which you will call A, B, C, and D. Then, you would say, "Point A on this image is located at (x2, y2), point B is located at (x2, y3)," and so forth. Then, simply instruct the drawer to connect the appropriate dots together to form the exact image. (Note: Choose the most appropriate measurement unit. For example, use inches if you are in interviewing in the U.S., but centimeters if you are interviewing in Canada. Alternatively, you could ask the drawer which system they are most comfortable with.)

Blinded tasks like this one, where one member of a team does not know what the final product should look like, are difficult and designed to test your communication skills and problem-solving skills. As a future professional, you will often have to make specialist knowledge accessible to non-specialists, so knowing how to break down a complex task or idea is a valuable skill. For a task-based station in your interview, bear in mind that, while the end result is important, the process itself is even more crucial. Using the approach outlined above will make you stand out amongst the other candidates. We recommend that you practice reproducing different types of images with friends and family prior to your interview so that you are fully aware of the potential difficulties that might arise during this process.

On your interview day, another candidate may be given the task of describing an image to you. As you reproduce the drawing or object, be sure to listen carefully to their instructions and politely ask for clarification, if needed. You may find that you have a difficult time reproducing the image because the other candidate is not using a very systematic method to describe it to you. If this happens, you may politely suggest that the other interviewee orient you to the bigger picture, or that they use the Cartesian system we have just described. Being able to tactfully assist your partner will highlight your leadership and teamwork skills and your capacity to remain calm and composed while engaged in a highly complex task. Displaying these qualities on your interview day will show the admissions committee that you are prepared for a career as a future medical professional.

We hope you now have a better understanding of the common question types as well as how to approach them. Remember, the best way to prepare for your interview is to not only learn about the question types theoretically, but to practice using the strategies yourself. You will have ample opportunities to do this in our later chapters that provide sample questions and answers, and full-length practice interview sets. But first, we want to give you some supplementary materials to this chapter so that you can better prepare for the questions to come, both in this book and during your actual interview!

CHAPTER VIII

Common Points of Debate in Medicine and Advanced Preparation Tactics

In this chapter, we give you some extra materials to aid you in your interview preparation. These include a) a list of controversial topics in the field of medicine, and b) ten additional preparation tips from our experts.

Major points of debate in medicine

Familiarizing yourself with the major points of debate in medicine will be valuable to your interview success. You may be asked about these topics directly in policy-based questions or even indirectly in scenario-type questions. Here are a few examples:

- Physician-assisted dying or end-of-life options

- Abortion
- Doctor or pharmacist prescribed birth control
- Vaccinations and whether they should be mandatory
- Legalization of recreational marijuana or other drugs
- Rural vs. urban healthcare
- Compulsory rural medicine service
- Stem cell research
- Genetic screening
- Prescribing medications to friends and family
- Allocation of finite resources (e.g. choosing which patient receives an organ transplant, which patient should receive the first surgery or the only dialysis machine)
- Prescription pain medication, over-prescription and addiction
- Safe injection sites and other harm reduction strategies to combat the opioid epidemic
- Vaping and regulations related to this activity
- Pass-fail vs. using grades to evaluate medical students
- Fee for service vs. salary and other compensation measures
- Obesity epidemic
- Other current issues in the U.S., Canada, Australia, New Zealand, Israel, the U.K., Europe or wherever you are going to have an interview

The list of topics we presented is not exhaustive of all major points of debates in healthcare. However, we provided you with a number of major topics. By staying up-to-date with these ongoing debates, you will acquire the knowledge necessary to address the issues presented to you in your interview. You can do this by reading the daily news and regularly visiting the websites or social media sites of your local or national professional associations such as the American Medical Association or Canadian Medical Association. Do not underestimate the time you need to spend reading and learning about such topics. This component of preparing for your interview should begin ASAP because crunching in the information at the last minute is not going to be sufficient. (Note that you will not be asked about academic topics like biology, chemistry, or physics. Schools have already evaluated your knowledge in these areas by looking at your GPA and MCAT score.)

Bonus Essential Preparation Tips

Here are a few final tips to help you prepare for your interview:

1. In the likely case that your interviewer asks you whether you have any questions for them, you must have a few prepared. This is not only an invaluable opportunity for you to learn more about the program, it is also your chance to demonstrate to the interviewers your commitment and interest in the program. A good question is one that a) you genuinely want to know the answer to, and b) is not obviously answered by the material available on the school website. Formulate your questions based on the thorough research you do on the program in advance. For example, after learning everything you can about the school, you may still have questions about the curriculum, upcoming or recent curricular changes, placements, rates of success for board examinations, research and teaching opportunities, extra-curricular activities, and so forth.

2. Be prepared to answer follow-up questions about any activity in your application – particularly if it is an open file interview format. You should be able to speak to each component of your application with ease.

3. Listen to yourself speak all the time. Are you overusing words and phrases such as "ummm", "like", "so", "because", "just", "honestly", "very", "really", "literally", "stuff", "you know", and "thing"? These words need to be eliminated from your vocabulary as they prevent you from coming across as professional, confident, clear, and succinct. We highly recommend that you review *It's the Way You Say It - Second*

Edition: Becoming Articulate, Well-Spoken, and Clear by Dr. Carol A. Fleming to learn how to become more articulate, a skill you need for life. We are not personally connected to this book or its author in any way (i.e. there's no conflict of interest in our plugging this book); we just genuinely find it to be one of the best resources out there for improving verbal articulation!

4. Be cognizant about not speaking ill of others, especially if you are trying to raise yourself up by putting others down. That will have the opposite effect of shedding negative light on yourself! Work on being positive and taking a positive approach to others at all times.
5. In addition to always shedding positive light on yourself and others, always finish each question with something positive, whether that is resolution to a conflict, a way that you grew through a difficult experience, or something that will help you in the future. *Never* end a response on a negative note. Recall how we talked about the primacy and recency effect. You do not want to end your response on a negative note because the last thing you say is what is going to be remembered most by the interviewers.
6. Take full responsibility for all your failures and weaknesses. It is not a bad thing to acknowledge failures or limitations. What medical schools look for is that you do not make excuses, but take ownership of your shortcomings. As noted above, end on a positive note by saying what you have done to overcome your failures or improve yourself.
7. When preparing for any question or question type, you want to say your answers out loud. Audio tape or video tape yourself, listen to what you said, and revise your response. You will be surprised how different it is to think of a response internally and then hear what you say when you verbalize it.
8. Take your interview seriously and your interviewers will take you seriously. The more preparation you put in using the advice in this book, the better you will perform. Your interviewers will be able to tell that that you prepared, and they will appreciate that you did not take this opportunity for

granted. This is a signal to the interviewers that you are ready to take on a professional role, work hard, and learn.

9. Remember you are being evaluated not only during the actual interview but during the whole day. Your interactions during the tour or while talking to medical students are also important. Medical students are often told by medical schools to be on the lookout for red flags or anything else concerning that candidates say during any part of the interview day. So, remember to stay 'on' the whole day; ask questions, be friendly to other applicants, and remain professional.
10. See the interview as an opportunity, not a barrier. Whereas the rest of your application is evaluated on paper or online, the interview is your chance to share about yourself and show your personality in-person. Take advantage of the interview and enjoy the experience!

We hope that the list of controversial topics and extra tips are helpful to you during your interview preparation. The main focus of the last two chapters has been on the structure and contents of your answers to interview questions. However, there are other non-verbal aspects of your interview that are equally important, but often missed by candidates! We are therefore eager to teach you these skills as well so that you can practice them simultaneously as you prepare for your upcoming interview.

CHAPTER IX

What to Wear, What to Say, and How to Communicate Non-verbally during Your Interview

At your interview, you will be judged on more than your responses to interview questions. Other aspects, such as your appearance and non-verbal behavior, are going to have a sure influence on how the interviewers view you as a candidate. We will go through these one by to help you prepare for and practice these along with your question responses.

Appearance

Let's begin with a discussion of your overall appearance. Studies have shown that the impressions formed within the first few seconds of meeting an interviewer can set the tone for the rest of the interview. Within this time frame, one of the most prominent things an interviewer will notice is how you dress. As such, you should make sure your attire and appearance are professional because you want to be remembered for your friendly personality and strong interview responses, not for your fashion choice or lack of hygiene!

For males, this means wearing a fitted grey, navy, or black suit with a plain white shirt, and a simple silk or silk-like tie. This should be paired with coordinating dark-colored dress socks and shoes. Jewelry other than watches and wedding rings should be kept to a minimum. You should have a fresh haircut and be clean-shaven or have neatly groomed facial hair.

Female candidates should wear a grey, navy blue, or black skirt or pant suit with a white or pastel button-down or pull-over blouse. If you choose to wear a skirt suit, ensure that the skirt comes down to at least the tops of your knees and no more than 2 to 3 inches above the knee while you are seated. Wear neutral-toned stockings and coordinating dark-colored closed-toe shoes that are comfortable. You will likely be walking around a lot on your interview day, and you will not want to be worrying about pain or blisters! Be conservative in your makeup application and aim for a neutral, everyday look. Jewelry should be understated and complement your overall outfit. For example, small stud earrings are more appropriate than large hoops. Your hair may either be worn up or down, as long as it is neat, professional, and does not obscure your face. You may find it preferable to wear your hair at least partially pulled back to avoid absent-mindedly touching it during the interview.

Some schools specifically request that their applicants not use any strongly scented products as the scent can be distracting and may cause allergic reactions in some sensitive individuals. Therefore, both male and female candidates should refrain from using perfume or cologne. Also be selective of the body washes and hair products you use as they may be too heavily scented.

Greetings and Goodbyes

As soon as you arrive on the premise, stay in tune with the individuals and happenings around you. You will be greeted by administrative staff, faculty members, students, and so forth, so don't let your interpersonal skills fall by the wayside. Smile, show excitement about being there, speak politely, and be pleasant with everyone you meet. Also, remember to interact with the other candidates who are there to be interviewed by engaging in light conversation about where they went to school, what they studied, and so forth. If you notice someone is really nervous, teach them some of the techniques you learned from this book. A professional always helps others, even their own competitors.

Once inside the interview room, make eye contact with the interviewer, smile, and offer to shake their hand. Make sure you have a nice firm grip and look the interviewer in the eyes as you say hello and introduce yourself. If the interviewer does not provide their name, it is appropriate for you to politely ask for it to help engage with the person. Of course, if they inform you that their policies do not allow them to share their names, simply accept the terms with a smile and say you understand. However, if they do tell you their name, ensure that you repeat their name. For instance, if your interviewer says, "Hello! I'm Dr. Johnson. It's nice to meet you!" You would reply, "Hello, Dr. Johnson. It is a pleasure to meet you!" This way you have made a mental note of their name. You can also consciously use their name a few times during the interview. This will come in handy once the interview is over, and you want to leave the best final impression. At this point, it is important that you shake your interviewer's hand again and thank them *by name* by saying something along the lines of, "Dr. Johnson, it was a pleasure speaking with you. Thank you for your time." By simply remembering your interviewers' names and thanking them prior to leaving the room, you will automatically set yourself apart from the candidates who do neither.

Your introduction and goodbye are extremely important to your overall interview performance. Assuming the interviewer pays equal attention to all parts of your interview, the initial and final moments of your interaction will still stand out disproportionately in your interviewer's memory because of the *primacy* and *recency effect*. As you may recall, the primacy effect is the tendency for people to remember earlier events better than latter events, while the recency effect dictates that people remember final events in more detail than events that occurred before. Additionally, there is scientific evidence showing that the magnitude of the primacy and recency effect is modulated by an individual's mood. If your interviewer is in a positive mood, the primacy effect may be magnified. If they are in a negative mood, the primacy effect will be reduced, and the recency effect will be increased in compensation. Regardless, there is no question that either your introduction or goodbye or both will make a lasting impression on the interviewer, so make the most of these two opportunities.

Non-verbal Communication

Of course, the rest of your interview will still matter a great deal. You must continue to demonstrate the strength of your candidacy through both verbal and non-verbal communication. Since we have discussed at length how to deliver strong verbal responses in previous chapters, we will now spend some more time talking about the non-verbal aspect of your interview.

By non-verbal, we mean what you are doing with your body as you speak. Above the shoulder, this includes maintaining eye contact to show engagement, showing appropriate emotions through facial expressions, and nodding to demonstrate your understanding and agreement with the other interlocuter. You should also refrain from laughing or smiling nervously, since this shows you lack confidence. From the shoulder down, this means your posture when sitting and also the positioning of your hands and feet. To ensure you have good posture, sit as far back in the chair as possible and straighten your back against the back of the chair. Next, place your feet flat on the ground and place your hands in your lap. Remember not to move around too much in your chair, clench your fists, or tap your toes. While it is okay to gesture here and there to facilitate delivery, refrain from overly grand gestures, touching your face, or playing with your clothes or hair. Just as confident positions alter your brain chemistry to make you feel confident, taking on stressed positions such as having crossed feet or sitting on your hands will also send stress signals to your brain. You can test this by holding one of these stress postures and paying close attention to changes in your physiology. You will likely observe your heart rate going up, body temperature increasing, and your hands beginning to feel clammy.

Non-verbal communication is important not only because the interviewer is paying close attention to it, but because it is largely subconscious and will more accurately reveal your inner mental state. Anytime the verbal and non-verbal messages contradict each other, your interviewer will likely believe the non-verbal message over the verbal one. For instance, if a candidate talks about caring for an individual who has suffered great loss, but their facial expression is blank and their tone of voice is flat, the interviewer will likely regard them as uncaring and uninterested. Overall, your body language accounts for up to 90% of your communication with others. Therefore, you must have excellent non-verbal communication to complement your verbal responses.

To summarize, here are the things you should and should not do in your non-verbal communication in point form. We begin with what you should do.

- Shake hands with your interviewer(s) when you say hello and when you say goodbye. The handshake should be firm but not crushing.
- Maintain eye contact to show confidence and engagement.
- Relax your face and smile. Show appropriate emotions at appropriate moments.
- Nod your head or say "Yes" to show that you are engaging in the conversation.
- Place both feet flat on the floor and relax your shoulders.
- Place your hands relaxed in your lap. Some gesturing may be appropriate if it helps you with your delivery.
- Project warmth, confidence, and interest with your tone of voice.

Here are the things you should refrain from doing:

- Don't touch your face or play with your hair as this may be interpreted as a sign of dishonesty.
- Don't slouch in your chair as this posture can make you seem disinterested.
- Don't cross your arms while sitting as it makes you seem defensive and/or disinterested.

- Don't fidget as this is distracting for the interviewer. Wringing your hands or tapping your feet will make you look nervous and uncomfortable.
- Don't laugh or smile nervously when you are unsure about a situation because it draws the interviewer's attention to your lack of confidence.

Considerations for Virtual or Video Interviews

Your appearance and communication are just as important for interviews conducted or recorded online. Do not make the mistake of slacking on any of the points above just because you are in the comfort of your home or office. You still need to communicate the same amount of commitment and professionalism as you would in an in-person interview! In fact, here are additional factors in an online or virtual interview setting that you must prepare for.

Internet connection:

You must ensure that you have a strong and stable internet connection for online interviews. If you know that your internet quality is poor, talk to your provider ahead of time about getting an upgrade, opt for using an ethernet cable instead of relying on WIFI, or ask a friend to use their internet for your interview. If you share bandwidth with others, let them know when you will be doing your interview and politely ask them to refrain from engaging in activities that take up a lot of bandwidth (e.g. streaming TV or gaming) during that time. You do not want to be disqualified over a technical difficulty you could have avoided.

Computer set-up:

You should use a desktop or laptop, not your smartphone. Consider the positioning and distance of your camera relative to your face and body. To encourage making eye contact and good posture, place your camera at eye-level. That way, you will be less inclined to stare above or below the screen as you speak, and you will be less likely to slouch in your chair. You should sit at a comfortable distance from your computer camera so that your upper torso is visible on screen. You don't want to appear on video as a floating head, and if you are someone who gestures with your hands, you will want those gestures to be visible. Use a high-quality microphone and check to make sure it is functioning properly. Lastly, be sure to exit all social media applications and websites on your computer and cellphone so that your interview is not disrupted by sound notifications and you are not distracted by occasional flashes on your screen.

Room set-up:

If your chair is on wheels and rotates, replace it with an immovable chair so that you are not tempted to turn or fidget during your interview as this would communicate a lack of confidence. The background that is visible on your screen should be fairly clean. We recommend doing the interview in front of a blank, neutral colored wall, or at least one that is minimally decorated. You do not want something in the background to distract the reviewer from your response. Also ensure that the lighting in the room is appropriate. You want your face to be well-lit with natural or natural-looking light from the side, rather than from above or behind. Both the background and lighting can significantly alter the reviewers' percept of you as a candidate, so they should not be taken lightly.

We highly recommend you test out these settings multiple times prior to your interview. If you know someone who will also be doing their interview in this format, we also encourage you to practice entire mock interviews with them over videoconferencing. Of course, this is exactly how we conduct mock interviews at BeMo, and students who participate in our interview preparation programs get tailored feedback about this from our experts!

In this chapter, we drew your attention to aspects of your interview that you may have never thought about, including your appearance, introductions and goodbyes, body language, and even the set-up for virtual interviews. While some of these, like what you choose to wear, can be easily managed, others, like your posture and tone of voice, can only be improved with much effort and time. However, all of these aspects will impact your interview score, particularly in categories to do with communication and suitability for the profession. Therefore, you must incorporate these elements into your preparation right from the beginning as you work on the delivery, structure, and contents to interview questions. Once again, we highly recommend that you get expert feedback, especially on your non-verbal communication, because these behaviors tend to be subconscious. An expert will not only be able to objectively point out behaviors that need to be corrected, but also teach you how to work on them.

We have now explored with you how to tackle interview questions of various types in terms of delivery, structure, and content. We have also shown you the details in your non-verbal communication you need to be aware of. If you are feeling overwhelmed by all of this information, or you begin to feel the mounting pressure as you start your interview preparation, we want you to know that a) this is normal given the colossal task you are about to tackle, and b) you can do something about it! In the next chapter, we will give you a number of strategies to help you manage your stress in the long-term and short-term, as well as on your interview day.

CHAPTER X

How to Manage Stress

One of the most common reasons good candidates fail their interviews is because they let their nerves get the best of them. Their sweaty hands are a huge turn-off to the receivers of the handshake, or they have a shaky voice, stumble over words, or cannot form coherent sentences. All of this translates into a perceived lack of confidence and poor communication skills.

Therefore, it is absolutely critical for you to develop strategies to cope with stress. These will help you for your interview and also for the rest of your professional and personal life. In this chapter, we are going to teach you both long-term and short-term strategies to manage your stress. We encourage you to experiment with all of them and choose the ones that work best for you.

Long-term Strategies

Let's begin by discussing some long-term solutions. These are strategies that you can begin to implement in the weeks and months leading up to your interview.

First, it goes without saying that going through the preparation process we have suggested, including familiarizing yourself with interview and question types, practicing in mock interviews, and getting expert feedback, will make you feel more at ease at your actual interview. The more realistic your practice is, the more comfortable you will be.

We also recommend that you visit the school to which you have been invited prior to your interview, and, if possible, ask to be taken around the campus by one of the current students. You can offer to pay for their time if you have to motivate them to help you explore the campus. The campus tour is extremely helpful for a few reasons. First, you can familiarize yourself with the interview site and surrounding area. That way, you will know exactly where you need to be and how to get there. We even recommend that you take multiple trips to and from the school and where you will be staying so you can figure out traffic patterns and any shortcuts. Immersing yourself in the campus environment and atmosphere will also put you at great ease on your interview day because being there will no longer be a novel experience. If you have time, engage in an enjoyable activity on campus close to the interview room, such as having a nice meal, listening to your favorite music, reading a book, or socializing with a friend. Furthermore, you may learn something new about the program by speaking to a current student, which may become useful for your interview. Ask them why they selected the school and what they find challenging about the program so that if you are asked similar questions during your interview, you will have another perspective to incorporate into your answer. If the interviewer knows you have spoken to current students to learn more about the program, they will be impressed by the amount of attention you are giving to this important life decision. However, we recommend that you avoid asking a current student for interview advice directly because a) they are still students and are not at a level to provide mentorship, and b) they actually don't know how well they did during their interview.

A number of schools have a day of activities planned for interviewees prior to the interview which includes a tour of the school. Though they are optional, we highly recommend that you participate as they are the perfect opportunity for you to see the campus, learn about the program, and possibly meet faculty, staff, and students at the school. Remember, while the admissions committee decides if you are a good fit for their institution, you are also deciding if the school is right for you. Considering that you are about to invest several years of your life in the program, you need to be happy with all aspects of the program, including non-academic factors such as school environment and location, access to gymnasium facilities, wellness programs, and so forth. You are choosing them as much as they are choosing you and this mind set will help you to remain confident.

Short-term Strategies

Having done everything you can to manage your stress in the long-term, you may still find that your stress levels rise shortly before your interview. This is normal, so here are some stress management strategies that you can draw upon in the days or hours leading up to your interview. Since different individuals conceptualize stress differently, each person will also find some coping mechanisms more effective than others.

Before we discuss healthy stress management strategies, we want to draw your attention to some unhealthy habits that may develop that will harm you in the long run. These include:

- Smoking
- Alcohol consumption
- Unhealthy eating (e.g. bingeing, not eating enough, overconsumption of caffeine or sugar)
- Self-isolation (i.e. withdrawing from or taking your stress out on friends and family, discontinuing hobbies, and so forth). Of course, if someone is the source of your stress, limiting the time you spend around that person will help.

- Sleeping too much or too little.
- Lack of or excessive exercise. A moderate amount of physical activity, such as weight training, running, swimming, and so forth, has proven psychological benefits like relieving stress. However, exercising to avoid other responsibilities, or over-exercising such that it results in drastic weight loss is not healthy.

Naturally, our recommendation is for you to avoid resorting to the above for stress relief. They are both ineffective and detrimental to your overall health.

Let's now discuss some healthy short-term stress management strategies that you can draw on, starting with what you can do to reduce anxiety and stress the night before your interview.

The night before your interview should *not* be spent reviewing or preparing for your interview. Cramming the night before or on the day of can have detrimental effects on your performance. By then, you should be well-prepared, so relax, enjoy, go to bed early, get a good night's sleep, and wake up early. The minute you wake up on the day of your interview, fill your mind with a positive thought, remind yourself of all the right things you have done in preparation for the interview, and think of the great opportunity that is ahead of you. If it helps, write yourself a motivational note the night before and read it in the morning. One positive thought in the morning can transform your whole day. Of course, take time to have a good breakfast, get ready, and give yourself ample time to travel to your destination. We recommend that you plan to arrive at your interview site at least 30 minutes before your interview is scheduled to begin. You should have mapped out several routes in advance so you know how long the commute will take and what other options you have if the primary route is unavailable due to traffic.

If you feel nervous before your interview, place a clean pen or pencil into your mouth horizontally and gently bite down on it with your back molars. This will force your facial muscles into a smile. Leave the pen or pencil in your mouth for about 2 minutes, take it out for a few minutes, and then repeat for another 2 minutes. Doing this will trick your brain into thinking that you are smiling, and the neurotransmitters that are released in this process will actually put you in a better mood and help you maintain a positive state of mind. The results are more apparent if you do it in front of a mirror. Alternatively, stand in front of the mirror and watch yourself smile. Your brain physiology will change, and you will begin to feel more positive. You can also try leaning back in a chair with your hands behind your head and your feet up, or standing with your arms outstretched, chest out, and head raised. As with the smiling exercise, you can trick your brain into thinking you are relaxed and confident by holding these positions for 30 seconds or more.

Breathing exercises also help to reduce stress. To do it effectively, take a deep breath in through your nose for 5 to 6 seconds, ensuring that you are using your diaphragm so that your belly puffs out, hold that breath for 4 seconds, and then exhale through your mouth for a prolonged 7 to 10 seconds, again using your diaphragm to push the air out. It should sound like an audible sigh as you breathe out. Repeat this a few times. The prolonged exhalation causes your parasympathetic nervous system to activate and simultaneously tones down your sympathetic nervous system. If you have access to a stethoscope, test this out by monitoring your heart rate as you perform this breathing exercise. As you take a deep breath in through your nose, notice your heart rate increasing. Then, exhale very slowly and notice your heart rate slowing down. This is actually how your doctor tests your sympathetic-parasympathetic tone. Prolonged diaphragmatic exhalation also occurs after a good laugh, cry, yawn, or sigh of relief, which is why you feel more relaxed after engaging in one of these gestures. This evolutionary tool has been harnessed by professionals such as basketball players who take a few deep breaths before shooting a free throw, or soccer players who do breathing exercises before taking a penalty kick. Military snipers are also trained to do breathing exercises before taking a shot because it reduces their heart rate and breathing rate to give them a more accurate shot. You also can take advantage of this evolutionary tool to aid your performance during your interview!

A few minutes before your interview begins, wash your hands with warm water and soap to get rid of any clamminess. It also helps to have a handkerchief in your pocket for wiping your hands before you enter the interview room.

We hope that some, if not all, of these long- and short-term stress management strategies will become useful for your as you gear up for your big day. Thus far, we have focused on what you should be doing before and during your interview. Thus, in the next chapter, we will complete the discussion by outlining what you should do *after* your interview, because contrary to what most people think, the application process does not end after you say goodbye to your interviewers!

CHAPTER XI

Post-mortem: What to Do After Your Interview

Before we dive into sample questions, let's complete our review of good interview etiquette by discussing what you should do after your interview. Most applicants miss these important steps because they think they are done once the interview is over, but there are a few things to do yet!

The #1 thing to do after your interview that's missed by 98% of applicants

It goes without saying that you should continue to smile and greet everyone around you as you leave the interview site, regardless of how you think your interview went. There is a good chance that you are still being watched by admissions staff and administrators, and you want to leave them with a great last impression of you.

The next and most important step is to spend time in self-reflection. Instead of calling your friends and family or celebrating, turn off your phone and find a quiet area to write down everything you remember from the moment you arrived on campus to the moment you left the interview. Record all the details ll the interactions you had, the questions you were asked, the answers you provided, the verbal and non-verbal cues you received from interviewers, and everything in between. You have about 30 minutes to do this before the adrenaline and the stress of the situation starts erasing or distorting your short-term memory. This is why detectives get trauma victims to sit down and explain exactly what happened as soon as possible, even if it means asking them to delay grievance. The exercise of self-reflection gives you the chance to record and learn from your mistakes so that you can do even better in the future.

The entire process of interview preparation, from beginning to end, will not only help you with medical school interviews, but also with residency and future job interviews. Furthermore, as a future professional, you will be habitually conducting a pre-mortem (what might go wrong) and post-mortem (what went wrong) to continuously refine your skills, no matter the field. As we said at the beginning of this book, our intent is not to teach you a few quick 'tricks' for you to ace your interview. You are honing important skills of critical thinking, communication, self-awareness, patience, perceptiveness, and so forth, skills that make you a better individual overall.

Communication with the School

After Your Interview

Overcommunication with the admissions committee after the interview is discouraged. If you are told that acceptances are given out after a specific date, it goes without saying that you should not call or email everyday beforehand to inquire about your admission status. Some schools will even explicitly tell you that they do *not* want ongoing communication or updates from applicants, so make sure you go through all of your existing emails from them to check if this is the case. If not, two forms of communication may be appropriate: thank-you notes and the letter of intent. Let's take a look at these in turn.

1. Thank-you notes

Consider sending a thank-you email 1 to 3 days after your interview. A note like this is especially appropriate if, during your interview, you had a meaningful conversation with your interviewer or panel. Note that this is merely an extension of good will; it will not sway the committee's decision.

If you choose to send one, your thank-you email should be written to the admissions committee, not individual interviewers. Address the email to the Dean of Admissions and either send it to the Dean directly or send it to the administrative assistant you have been communicating with thus far. The email does not have to be long and drawn out. Simply express your gratitude for the opportunity to be considered and your anticipation about your potential future at the school. If you had a memorable conversation, briefly describe what it was about. The following is a template:

> Dear Dr. __________ (name of the Dean of Admissions)
>
> Thank you very much for giving me the opportunity to interview at __________ (school name) on __________ (date). I particularly enjoyed chatting about __________ (topic of discussion) with Dr. __________ (name of the interviewer) and learning more about your program. This experience only highlighted how excited I am at the prospect of attending medical school at __________ (school name).
>
> Please let me know if there is anything else I can send to support my application.
>
> Sincerely,
> __________ (your name)

2. Letter of Intent

Unlike a thank-you email, the letter of intent is a document that can absolutely have a positive impact on your application. This is a *single* letter sent to *one* school, your top choice, stating that you will accept their offer of admission over and above any other schools you have applied for, even if you have already been admitted to another school. Please note that you *cannot* send such a letter to all the schools you have interviewed for because they cannot all be your top choice. Doing so would be dishonest and unethical, and it will create an extremely awkward situation should you receive multiple acceptances.

The best time to send the letter of intent is about a month after your interview, especially if you have been waitlisted at your top choice school. If you are interviewing at multiple schools, you may want to wait until you have completed a few of your interviews and considered all the options available to you.

As you will be declaring that this school is your #1 choice, your letter must be sincere, you must demonstrate that you have weighed all the options, and the reasoning behind your choice must be laid out clearly and concisely. The entire letter, including the address and your signature, should span at most a page. This is a formal letter, so needless to say, your grammar and spelling must be impeccable. Address and send your letter to the Dean of Admissions, the person who will be making the final decisions regarding admissions. The following is an outline of what you should include in your letter:

Opening:

- Address the addressee by their full name and title.

Paragraph 1:

- Give a self-introduction, including your full name, your status as a current applicant to the program, and the date of your interview.
- Establish that the school as your top choice, clearly stating that you *will* attend their school if you are offered admission into their program.

- If you have already received another offer, state that even though you have been accepted to that school, this school remains your top choice and you will attend if you are extended an offer of acceptance.

Paragraph 2:

- Provide your genuine reasons for making this school your top choice. You can discuss what aspects of their program, curriculum, research, or vision stand out to you and why these are central to your decision.
- Demonstrate why you are an ideal candidate by discussing ways you could uniquely contribute to their program and campus community.

Paragraph 3 (optional):

- Provide any updates since submitting your application and interviewing. This might include upcoming plans, new publications, upcoming conference presentations, awards, and so forth.

Closing:

- Reiterate your interest in their program.
- Sincerely thank them for taking the time to review your letter.
- Sign off formally with "Sincerely,", "All the best,", or something similar and your full name.
- If you are a U.S. applicant, include your AAMC ID number beneath your name.

You can send the letter as an email or as a PDF attachment to your email. The subject line should be your full name followed by "Letter of Intent".

The bottom line is that schools want to admit students who are motivated, proactive, and enthusiastic about being there. If you are certain that one program is best suited to your needs, interests, and passions, then reach out to them and make your preference known!

Now that we have outlined the dos and don'ts of the medical school interview process from preparation to post-interview etiquette, we can finally begin to practice! To ease you into this, *Chapter XII: 20 Sample Medical School Interview Questions with Expert Responses* provides you with sample interview questions with sample answers and discussions. *Chapter XIII: 100 Practice Medical School Interview Questions* then gives you additional questions to practice everything you have learned so that you can better internalize the strategies and get a feel for timing and flow.

Are you ready? Let's go!

CHAPTER XII

20 Sample Medical School Interview Questions with Expert Responses and Analyses

In this chapter, you will find 20 difficult interview questions, each with an example of a weak response, a strong response, and an expert analysis of these responses.

Throughout the answers, you will see bracketed annotations pointing out the use of different components of the structures and strategies we discussed in *Chapter VII: Proven Strategies to Approach and Ace Any Medical School Interview Question*. You may notice that the strong answers are longer and contain more information than what you might actually include in a real interview response. We did this intentionally to show you a variety of points you *could* discuss in your answer and to help you learn as much as possible during your preparatory process. However, remember that you should be giving concise answers during your actual interview.

After giving examples of a weak and strong answer, we will then discuss the rationale behind the answers, focusing on what was weak or strong about each response.

To get the most out of these practice questions and answers, we recommend you answer each question yourself first, then evaluate your response against our weak and strong answers.

Question 1: Tell me about yourself.

Weak response:

I was born and raised in a small town in Michigan. I went to St. George's High School and did very well, so I applied to college and was lucky to get into University of Michigan for undergrad (lack of elaboration). In college, I finished pre-med (**no reasoning behind why candidate chose to study this**) and decided to go to medical school, so here I am applying and interviewing for medical school admission. I am very hard working and dedicated to what I do, and I also enjoy other extracurricular activities such skiing, running, and hanging out with friends (**does not give evidence to back up skills mentioned or expand on extracurriculars**).

Strong response:

Thank you for the opportunity to share a bit about myself. The important things to know about me stem from what I value most in life: family and friends, music, and advocacy for those who don't have a voice of their own (**clear introduction**).

I grew up in a small town near Dayton, Ohio, surrounded by family and friends, but it wasn't until I left for college in New York that I realized just how important they were to me. I had a difficult transition from rural to city life (**identifies a meaningful experience and challenge**). During that time, my biggest source of support was from my parents and friends from back home. When I was feeling down, they would cheer me up over Skype or send me messages of encouragement. When I finally acclimatized to my environment, they sent me care packages to help me get over my academic hurtles (**discusses how the challenge was overcome with examples**). Through this experience, I realized how vital their support was for my success and my mental health, and I began to see a need for this kind of support amongst my classmates and in my campus community (**highlights the significance of this experience**).

So, I started a wellness program for students at my college, using music as my inspiration (**identifies a second impactful experience**). I've been involved in music my entire life. As a child, I learned piano, and I eventually started playing the clarinet in orchestra and jazz band. The greatest thing about the arts is that it allows you to connect with like-minded, but diverse people, and for me especially, playing music was a great way to manage my stress (**highlights take-aways**). To bring these benefits to my college community, I started organizing music socials for freshmen, and I collected and redistributed used instruments to those who wanted to play but couldn't afford to. Many of the members who got involved were transitioning students who later told me that participating in the program not only helped them overcome the initial challenges of living in New York, but they also made life-long friends in the process (**demonstrates proactive approach and community service**). Music will definitely continue to be a big part of my life, but I was especially glad to have shared it with others in a way that made a positive impact on them (**summarizes the impact of the experience**).

However, what challenged and changed me the most in this experience was the people I met (**transitional statement to ensure flow**). I had the opportunity to connect with amazingly talented musicians from all walks of life, including international students, single parents, people who were returning to school after having a career, and so forth. One of these, in particular, was a Dreamer who had to overcome unimaginable cultural, financial, and political barriers just to attend college, and now lives in constant fear of deportation (**describes a significant interaction**). I was so moved by his story that I decided to join the Dreamer advocacy group on campus to take part in this movement, which aims to protect these vulnerable, but equally important, members of our society. We routinely call our senators to discuss DACA and surrounding policies, and we hold regular seminars on campus to educate the community on these issues. As I continue to be an active member of this group, I've started to research other underrepresented and underserved populations in New York City to learn what I can do for them as well (**highlights advocacy**). As someone who comes from privilege, I feel it is my responsibility to lend my voice to those who do not have a voice of their own (**future application**).

These three areas – family and friends, music, and advocacy – have, at various points, become integral parts of my life (**summarizes the points discussed**). I am constantly learning how to support those around me in the same way that my loved ones have supported me. I also remain committed to serving my community through music, advocacy, and in the future, my expertise in medicine (**future application**).

Discussion:

This is one of the most commonly asked questions during medical school interviews. It is important to be well-prepared for this question and present your life story in a structured and interesting way. A common mistake that candidates make is listing their experiences in a CV form without any explanation, like in the *weak* response. We recommend that you, instead, take the interviewer through three of your most meaningful experiences in chronological order, as in the *strong* response, highlighting the turning points and important events that have shaped you to be the person you are today. These experiences may or may not be medical, but they should all demonstrate personal characteristics that are valuable for a future physician. The key to answering this question is to *show* rather than just *tell*. Focus on a smaller number of experiences and give specific examples to demonstrate what you learned from each of them.

Question 2: Why did you decide to go into medicine?

Weak response:

I decided to go into medicine because I truly enjoy taking care of people and providing them with the best treatments possible. I also really like working in a team and I think I will be a good fit for this profession in the future. My parents are also physicians and I was introduced to medicine early. Considering all my previous experiences, I would love to treat people and be a knowledgeable physician in the future (**student has simply stated facts without any evidence**).

Strong response:

Thank you for asking this very important question. There are many reasons why I would like to enter the medical field, but I would like to discuss the three most important ones in my life (**clear introduction**).

Firstly, I grew up in a medical family where my parents, both physicians, had to take care of me and my sister as well as their patients in the hospital. My parents taught me the importance of passion, dedication, and commitment to the medical field and other human beings. Despite, their limited time with me, they exemplified these traits every day and were always role models to me and my sister. My childhood and experiences associated with it definitely sparked my interest in medicine (**identifies first exposure to medicine**).

Secondly, the experiences that I had as a student, researcher, and volunteer have shaped the curiosity and knowledge-seeking attitude that I live by every day. One particular experience from my senior undergraduate year stands out to me (**uses an example to show, not just tell**). I witnessed a pedestrian get hit by car and, as a result, had a bleeding laceration on his arm. Even though I was just a student at the time, I used my knowledge from my recently completed "Stop the Bleed" class to provide the initial care and tamponade his bleeding until the paramedics arrived. The ambulance team thanked me for what I did and told me that I might have saved his life (**concise description of experience in 3 sentences**). This experience made me realize that medical knowledge paired with a sense of responsibility toward fellow human beings is what medicine is all about. At that moment, I realized that this is the profession I would like to dedicate my life to (**highlights what the experience taught them**).

Last but not least, I would like to emphasize the importance of research in my life. I have had the opportunity to be part of excellent research teams in the fields of surgical oncology and trauma surgery. They both taught me problem-solving and communication skills that will help me not only help individual patients, but also benefit the larger population by engaging in groundbreaking research. The opportunity to evaluate large datasets, analyze tumor tissue in the lab, or conduct BLS classes for other medical providers have further taught me the importance of research in medicine and looking at the big picture (**highlights lessons learned and why these skills are key to the practice of medicine**).

All these activities and experiences have shaped me to be an ambitious, dedicated, and proactive medical professional who will dedicate their career to helping patients in a time of need, whether it is in the operating room, clinic, or on the street (**concluding sentence to summarize answer**).

Discussion:

This is another commonly asked question during interviews for medical school. The interviewers often want to know your personal reasons for entering this specific profession. In the *weak* answer, the candidate lists three reasons but does not instantiate each of them with a specific example. In contrast, the *strong* response focuses on the three most important events or experiences that have defined the candidate as a medical applicant. Try to always think about the events that have made you realize why you would like to enter this field and how they exemplify strong personal characteristics for medical applicant. These may include dedication, passion, perseverance, curiosity, and so forth. Of course, it is important to show these characteristics through examples and to discuss your experiences in chronological order so the interviewer can follow your thought process and clearly see your growing interest over time.

Question 3: Why would you like to attend our medical school?

Weak response:

This is a great school because of the early clinical exposure and the research opportunities (**statements made without supporting details**). I also like that students get great results on their board exams and have a high chance of matching to specialties, so coming here will help me succeed (**response focuses on self-gain**).

Strong response:

Thank you for asking this question. I put a lot of thought into where I applied as there are many wonderful medical schools (**indicates research done**). However, in looking into your program, I feel I would be a great fit here for 3 reasons. First, I really like the clinical exposure that occurs early on in the first year of the program. I myself learn best when theory is combined with practical experience. For example, I really enjoyed my 4th year biochemistry lab as it allowed me to apply the theories I learned in lecture to the experiments we conducted, thereby cementing my knowledge. Coming to a school with this type of curriculum will help me become the best physician I can be (**provides reason based on curriculum**). Secondly, this program is invested in innovative research. I have done research on the social isolation of the elderly under the supervision of Dr. Greer at my university. Seeing as there are labs in your school that also carry out this line of research, I would love to continue it here and contribute what I know to this area (**provides reason based on extracurricular opportunities, also adds something they can contribute to program**). Lastly, I would love to live in this diverse city. I feel the multicultural population and multitude of clinical settings will give me exposure to the widest population range and help me become a stronger physician who understands the different needs of my patients (**provides reason based on location**). I look forward to studying here!

Discussion:

Just like for questions such as "Tell me about yourself" and "Why are you pursuing a career in medicine?", your answer for this question needs to be focused and personal. The *weak* response gives two vague descriptors of the program, but no details to show the candidate has actually done any serious research. The candidate also focuses on how they can benefit from the school without also highlighting ways in which they can contribute back. In the *strong* response however, the candidate discusses each point in detail and relates the school's attribute to themselves, making the reasons unique and personal. They also suggested a way in which they can make a positive contribution to the program and show that they are committed to the community.

As you research your schools, go beyond the first page of the program's website and read about their curriculum in detail. Try to speak to a current student if you can. Once you have thoroughly researched the program, identify 2 to 3 meaningful reasons you wish to study there. For each reason, provide an example or anecdote relaying exactly why that aspect of the curriculum resonates with you and makes you a great fit for their program. The level of dedication and enthusiasm your show for their program in an answer like this will impress the interviewers.

Question 4: What is your biggest limitation?

Weak response:

I think my biggest limitation is the fact that I do not know how to say "no" to people and often take on too many projects. I keep myself involved in many different organizations and the responsibilities often become too much for me (**mentions a limitation that is not a true weakness and does not provide any examples**). I think it is important to remain active on different levels and therefore I continuously work to finish everything on time (**does not provide specific details of how this limitation was overcome**).

Strong response:

I believe one of my limitations is the tendency to procrastinate (**mentions a true limitation**). When I was studying for my final exams during my freshman and sophomore years of college, I would postpone my studying until the week before the finals. Even though I have always performed well on the final exams, I was unable to retain much of the knowledge I learned (**provides specific example to show impact on their life**).

I realized that I needed to build a solid knowledge base before medical school, as every physician should strive to continuously learn and use that knowledge in practice. Since my sophomore year, I have implemented significant changes in my studying habits, including setting short-term study goals, having designated study hours, and using Google calendar reminders to keep myself on track (**provides specific examples of solutions**). Since I implemented these changes, I have been able to achieve a higher GPA, a competitive MCAT score, and more importantly, a solid knowledge base that I feel confident about. This experience has taught me the importance of preparation, systematic learning, and persistence in excelling and reaching my goals. I will certainly continue to strive for excellence while in medical school (**highlights lessons learned and future plans to combat limitation**).

Discussion:

The reviewers often want to know how you perceive your weaknesses and strengths. Thus, this is a personal-type question that is commonly asked during interviews. For this question, it is important to identify a true limitation, as the candidate does in the *strong* response. If you try to disguise a strength as a weakness, as in the *weak* response, it will be impossible for you to discuss the heart of this question, which is what you have done to *overcome* your limitation. After you have briefly described a true weakness and why it is limiting, focus your response on the specific changes you made in your life to work on your weakness. Be sure to provide examples of how you have improved and where you are in terms of progress. All responses to personal type questions must be supported with specific personal examples. Otherwise, you risk your answer being disingenuous.

Question 5: Can you tell me about a time when you had to disagree with your superior?

Weak response:

I usually don't disagree with my supervisors, but one time my PI and I did have different opinions on a political topic. During the discussion, I told him that I don't support his views and I decided to avoid him for a month because of that (**does not give specific details of what the disagreement was about and shows immaturity in dealing with this situation**). The following days when I had to interact with him, I would come up with an excuse that I had other responsibilities. I consider my beliefs to be important for me and I stand behind them regardless of who is on the other side (**does not consider superior's point of view**).

Strong response:

The medical field is a stressful environment and conflicts happen, even with superiors. I once disagreed with my Principal Investigator (PI) about some research results during a lab meeting (**uses specific details to show, not tell**). I was the person in charge of the experiment on the levels of different cytokines in cancer patients. Despite thorough preparation and analysis of my data, the PI stated that the data I presented did not make sense to him and was not worth presenting anywhere (**concisely describes the conflict**). Although I value his opinion a lot, I truly believed that my results were worthwhile and therefore I decided to discuss it with him in person. I prepared a PowerPoint presentation showing a review of the literature followed by the results and highlighted what these results told us about the hypotheses we established at the beginning of the project. I was very polite, informative, and receptive to feedback. At the end of the conversation, my PI explained to me that he was just having a bad day and he apologized for what transpired that day (**shows reflection and maturity in response**). He agreed that the results were excellent, and I offered him further support if he ever needed a break from our stressful work environment (**shows empathy for superior**). This situation taught me that it is important to stand behind your work if you feel it is valuable. It also showed me that even the most educated and experienced individuals can have off days, and that I can help them during their time of need (**highlights lessons learned and future application**).

Discussion:

This is a different personal-type question where you are asked to discuss a conflict you had with a superior. For any such questions, the interviewer is looking for an example that demonstrates your conflict resolution abilities. While the *weak* response demonstrates a lack of maturity and inability to consider multiple perspectives, the *strong* response shows that the candidate is willing to communicate and be empathetic to other parties involved in the conflict. When you answer this question or questions like this, be sure to clearly and concisely describe a situation where you were in that position, then give details about how you approached the situation. Choose an example where your response to the conflict was polite and non-confrontational, and where you considered the other person's perspective. This will show the interviewer that you are a mature individual who is able to effectively de-escalate tense situations that may arise in your future professional life.

Question 6: What kind of superpower would you like to have and why?

Weak response:

I can't really think of any superpowers that I would like to have. I like the way I am right now (**does not answer the question**).

Strong response:

This is a very interesting question. Please let me take a couple seconds to think about it before I answer (**an applicant can pause for a few moments to gather their thoughts**). Based on my experiences, the superpower I would like to have most is the ability to teleport in time and space (**answers the question clearly by stating a superpower**). The reason I picked this superpower is because I often find myself in situations where I would like to be in two places at once. For example, I have limited time on weekends, and I am forced to choose between spending it with my family or my friends. If I had this superpower, I would be able to spend time with both groups of people who are very important to me. Additionally, I have a lot of family in Europe and we rarely get to see each, therefore having the ability to teleport would be amazing as we would be able to see each other more often. I would be able to attend all the family events and re-unions that I miss each year. Furthermore, I never had an opportunity to meet my grandmother who passed away when I was 2 years old. I have always wondered what kind of person she was and the ability to teleport in time would give me the opportunity to meet her and get to know her (**clearly and concisely describes three reasons why this particular superpower is desired**).

Discussion:

This is a quirky-type question, which usually asks you to discuss a seemingly random topic, catching you off guard. In the *weak* response, the candidate either dismissed the question, thinking it's unimportant, or they were unable to think on their feet and come up with an answer. Needless to say, you must actually answer the question, rather than dodge it completely. If you are indeed caught by surprise, it's ok to take a few seconds to think about the best answer before you begin to respond, as the candidate did before giving the *strong* response. This is your chance to show your creativity, not to mention your ability to respond under pressure. In order to answer this particular question well, you must not only pick a superpower, but also justify your choice. Again, your reasons must be personal, and with each one, you should aim to share a personal trait with the interviewer that they would otherwise not know.

Question 7: What would you do if you were not selected this admission cycle?

Weak response:

I have not really thought about this possibility (**shows that the applicant has not taken all outcomes into consideration**), but I will probably continue to work with my current employer and do more research during this gap year to improve my chances in the future. However, I think my chances of admission this year are pretty decent (**shows overconfidence and naivety**).

Strong response:

This is a very important question as it is always important to account for the possibility of failure and plan for alternative routes to achieve one's goals (**shows understanding that medicine is a competitive field and that admission is not guaranteed**). If I am not granted admission this cycle, I would certainly reflect on the potential mistakes I made and identify any imperfections in my application (**takes a non-judgmental approach and reflects on own mistakes**). I would search for an advisor or consultant who could point out my weaknesses so I can improve them for the next cycle (**proactively seeks out expert feedback**). Additionally, I would continue to expand my scientific and clinical knowledge by continuing my immunology research with Dr. Johnson and shadowing at the Children's Hospital of Toronto. I will likely try to expand my volunteer appointments to learn more about the community where I would like to serve as a physician in the future. Through these experiences, I will gain more exposure to both clinical medicine and the social difficulties that these populations are facing with the hopes of serving them better in the future (**highlights experiences the candidate will pursue and why these will prepare them for a career in medicine**). I understand the road to a desired career in medicine can be difficult, but I am committed to this journey and I will continue to grow as an individual to meet the requirements of a medical professional (**states commitment to field of medicine**).

Discussion:

Though this is a commonly asked question, candidates, like the one who gave the *weak* response, often do not have an appropriate answer prepared. You must not only outline a tangible game plan, but in doing so, you must also show your dedication to this profession despite possible failure initially. As in the *strong* response, provide specific examples of activities you will continue, then discuss how you would like to expand your experiences to gain a wider perspective on the profession. Be sure to detail how these engagements will enrich your understanding of the role of health care professionals and how they will better prepare you to become a future physician.

Question 8: What do you think is the most pressing issue in medicine in the U.S./Canada?

Weak response:

In my opinion, the biggest problem is with insurance companies (**does not acknowledge the many issues in health care**). Patients don't have enough money to cover their medical expenses and often end up having huge debts (**a sweeping statement that does not discuss the nuances of the issue**). I think physicians should be aware of that because it is important to distinguish between those who have insurance and who don't (**a non-solution to the issue, physicians know whether their patients have insurance**). Also, people with insurance will have a better chance of receiving good care in the hospital versus the ones without insurance, which could also be a problem (**makes statement without providing evidence**). This is just one example, but there are many problems we are facing.

Strong response:

Thank you for this interesting question. There are a number of difficulties that our health care system is facing right now (**acknowledges other possible answers**). One of the major issues is access to health care in the rural setting. Growing up in a small town in Michigan, some members of my family were not able to access the specialized health care they needed (**states an issue and uses personal experience to showcase it**). When my grandfather was diagnosed with pancreatic cancer, he needed a highly specialized Whipple surgery to remove his tumor, but the closest pancreatic surgeon was 300 miles away and it took him over three months to schedule an appointment. Since pancreatic cancer is a progressive cancer, he found out that it was too late to operate at the time of initial consultation. This demonstrates that the access to health care is absolutely necessary for all members of the society and we as physicians should think of the best ways to provide this access. I have personally engaged in a local health care advocacy support group at the local governmental office to voice these concerns on behalf of patients (**states a solution and demonstrates experience with helping to alleviate the problem**). Pursuing medicine will give me further opportunities to fight for access in underserved communities (**states that their advocacy will continue in their future career**).

Discussion:

The discussion about health care issues is common among physicians and health care professionals. Since no system is perfect, there are a number of issues that could be discussed and should be acknowledged. However, in the *weak* response, the candidate hastens to single out one problem without any reasoning behind their choice, then proceeds to make unsupported points and does not propose any real solutions. Rather than simply expressing your broad views, it is more effective to focus on the issues that you feel most strongly about or that you have personal experience with, as in the *strong* response. It is always valuable to provide an example that brings you closer to the issue you identify. Always explore tangible solutions that aim to solve the problem directly, and where possible, propose how you would personally work to alleviate the issue. To prepare for such questions and facilitate discussion, stay up to date with current healthcare policies and issues.

Question 9: Consider the following scenario. You are a medical student on your surgical rotation. You are supposed to scrub in on a case with a senior attending surgeon, but he is late to the pre-op area. When he arrives, he appears to be unsteady on his feet and smells strongly of alcohol. The team was scheduled to start the case in 15 minutes. How would you handle this situation?

Weak response:

In this situation, I would probably talk to the attending surgeon right away and ask him whether he had been drinking alcohol (**confrontational, judgmental approach**). I would also tell him that it is inappropriate to show up to work under the influence. Since I am only a medical student in this situation, I would not take any serious actions since it is not my role to make decisions here, but maybe if it happens again, I would report him to the chair of the department (**appears to step back from wanting to get involved unless directly impacted, does not consider impact on others**).

Strong response:

In this specific scenario, my primary concern is for the safety and well-being of our patients (**states the pressing issue and identifies vulnerable parties**). I am also concerned about the well-being of the physician since he might have alcohol-related issues. However, I would not jump to any conclusions before I gathered some more information (**takes a non-judgmental approach**). I would talk to the surgeon privately and first ask him if he's okay. I would then calmly and non-confrontationally tell him what I had observed and ask him why he was late, stumbling, and smelled of alcohol. I would also try to determine whether this is a one-time occurrence or if it is a recurring issue (**gathers evidence**). If, through this conversation, I find out that there were independent reasons for him being late, stumbling, and smelling like alcohol, that these have nothing to do with alcohol consumption and he is perfectly sober and able to operate, I would simply explain the source of my confusion and tell him that my concern was for his well-being as well as that of the patient. If I find out that the surgeon is under the influence, unable to operate, and potentially in need of medical attention, I would inform the rest of the team so that they can immediately try to minimize the impact this has on the patient by finding another surgeon to operate, or, in the worst case, rescheduling the surgery. I would then make sure that the surgeon got the medical attention or rest he needs to recover, and later have a discussion with him about how to prevent such a thing from reoccurring in the future. If I find out that the surgeon is under the influence, and this is a recurring issue, I would do what I can to get him the support he needs. However, whether it was a one-time occurrence or not, if there is an issue with being under the influence on the job, I would have to report the incident to the chair of the department so the they can evaluate the danger this poses to our patients and other team members and take action if need be (**describes multiple hypotheticals and clearly outlines response to each situation**). In summary, I would remain objective, and focus on gathering as much information as I can about the situation without jumping to conclusions. With our patients' safety and well-being as my top priority, I would provide appropriate solutions based on the evidence I have (**provides a brief summary of answer**).

Discussion:

This is a typical scenario-type question, which is most common in MMI type interviews, but will often show up in traditional interviews as well because they can reveal a lot about a candidate's character and their ability to respond to complex situations under pressure. In the *weak* response, the candidate simultaneously takes a confrontational approach and takes a step back from their responsibility toward the safety of their patients. In contrast, the candidate who gives the *strong* response approaches their superior calmly and maturely, and also involves themselves in the multiple solutions they offer, taking responsibility for both their patient and their colleague. A lot of candidates jump to conclusions and provide their own opinions in the beginning of the answer, but it is important to remain non-judgmental and objective. To do this, you must first identify the pressing issue, then gather the missing information, provide several hypothetical scenarios and solutions, and summarize your approach.

By following this structure, you will be able to provide a systematic, step-by-step answer that is easy for the interviewer to follow.

Question 10: What do you think about legalizing marijuana in certain states and countries?

Weak response:

I don't think this is a good idea, because a lot of people will abuse it and the consequences associated with this can be tragic (**jumps straight into opinion without any discussion of the topic or pros and cons**). For example, a lot of people will overdose and end up in the hospital or they will drive while intoxicated, which is dangerous. I have always been against the legalization of marijuana and I don't think it should be allowed for any reason (**close-minded, judgmental approach**).

Strong response:

This is an important topic and policy to discuss, especially with the many existing viewpoints among different groups in our society (**demonstrates awareness of topic**). There are certainly some advantages to legalizing marijuana, especially when it comes to medical applications. There have been scientific case studies of patients with severe headaches, neurological disorders, and a number of mental health disorders who have been able to better manage their conditions with medical marijuana. Legalizing marijuana would also allow the government to tax it, generating revenue which can then be cycled back into healthcare and other systems in need of funding. Furthermore, legalizing marijuana will allow agencies like the FDA to monitor and ensure the quality of the product. On the other hand, there are also disadvantages associated with it, including the potential abuse of marijuana. Intoxication related to marijuana could lead to impaired driving, lack of judgment, and even neurological deficits (**describes both pros and cons to the policy**). Considering the pros and cons of this policy, I personally disagree with the broad legalization of marijuana across entire states or countries because of the significant risks listed above and the lack of individualized protocols for the use of medical marijuana. However, I do believe this is a topic that should continue to be researched by physicians and scientists, and evidence-based options that could benefit patients should be systematically evaluated (**states personal opinion clearly**

alongside reasoning, and also highlights next steps to continue evaluating the policy).

Discussion:

This is a typical policy-type question that asks you to discuss your views on a policy or current issue. The interviewers would like to see whether you have the knowledge base to effectively evaluate a new or controversial policy or issue. Remain objective and analytical in the beginning of your answer, as in the *strong* response, rather than leading with your personal opinion, as in the *weak* response. The appropriate steps are to first acknowledge the importance of the issue and recognize who it impacts the most, then discuss the advantages and disadvantages, making sure to present sound arguments for each side. Once you have weighed both sides, state your personal opinion about the issue. You can also suggest any alternatives and modifications and discuss future considerations regarding the issue to show that you have a broader outlook. Though you will not be evaluated based on the 'correctness' of your opinion, you must keep up to date with the current healthcare policies to be able to formulate valid arguments.

Question 11: What was your most valuable experience during your undergraduate education and why?

Weak response:

My most valuable experience was participating in a fraternity during my undergraduate years. It definitely showed me how to deal with social issues and other people within the group. We often worked as a team and organized a lot of different social events. This experience was a lot of fun, but it also taught me a number of life skills (**vague response with no supporting details**).

Strong response:

I had a number of valuable experiences during my time at University of Iowa, but the one I find most rewarding was the Global Medicine Initiative Project where I had the opportunity to be one of the executive board members and organizers (**clearly states experience, organization, and role**). It was a project that provided medical care and resources to low-income populations in Africa. Our responsibility was to collect medical supplies from the hospitals and medical centers here in New York and arrange transport and delivery to African countries in need, including Sierra Leone, Ghana, and the Democratic Republic of Congo. As one of the co-founders of this initiative, I had the opportunity to travel to several of these countries and see how much the local population appreciated the medical supplies. The resources we provided them often allowed them to provide care to thousands of children, mothers, and elderly people. The image of a happy child after a simple antibiotic treatment for sinusitis will always stay with me (**uses specific details to describe experience**). This opportunity has taught me a number of valuable lessons. The importance of teamwork and organization within the group was the main reason we succeeded in this project and I therefore considered myself lucky to have led such a talented group. Additionally, I learned the importance of community service and was humbled by the endless appreciation that these vulnerable people have for the small amount of relief that we provided (**describes the lessons learned**). It allowed me to see the impact I can make and encourages me to continue participating in global medicine missions in the future (**ends with future application**).

Discussion:

Questions regarding your memorable experiences in college are common. Although it does not matter whether you discuss a medical or non-medical experience, it is important to discuss the lessons you have learned, skills you have acquired, or personal characteristics that you displayed. In the *weak* response, the candidate identifies an experience and some skills they learned. However, the example of their involvement is too vague for the interviewer to gauge whether or not they truly exhibited those skills, and it is difficult to appreciate why this experience was valuable. In the *strong* response on the other hand, the candidate provides ample detail of their role in a specific organization and project, and it is clear what the impact of the project was on the candidate and the communities they worked with, thus making it easy to understand why they chose to discuss this particular experience. We encourage you to select experiences in which you to served others or came to a deeper understanding of the needs of others. These include, but are not limited to community service, volunteer work, and shadowing experiences. Be sure to justify your choice and describe a specific observation or interaction that was especially impactful to make the experience tangible to the interviewer. Then discuss the take-aways and future application.

Question 12: Which organ would you be in the body and why?

Weak response:

Wow, what a tough question! I would be the brain. It's so intricate and complex, and I love learning more about the brain! (**brief, shallow, candidate misses the opportunity to tell the interviewer about their own character**).

Strong response:

If I had to be an organ, I would choose to be the liver because it can withstand assault from toxins and even regenerate itself! I feel like I am vulnerable, like every other person, but, like the liver, I have learned to be resilient too (**focuses not on the organ, but on their own personal trait**). In one of my busiest years in undergrad, I lost my grandfather to lung cancer. I was very close to my grandpa and thought I would fall apart, but I asked for help and support from family, friends, and my university during this difficult time. I was able to take a step back from studying for a few days and really mourn my grandpa with our loved ones. Though it was hard to return to my studies after experiencing this loss, I was also determined to do everything I could to contribute to the lifesaving field of medicine, and I wanted to make my grandpa proud. With this as my motivation, I got back on track, and with the help of my TAs and professors, I was still able to complete all of my courses in good standing (**uses real example to showcase resilience**). I believe this experience prepares me for the stressful times ahead, especially as I face challenges while studying medicine. I feel confident that I can reach out for help and overcome obstacles with the same resilience in the future. (**looks ahead to future application**).

Discussion:

When asked a quirky question, it is easy to just supply the most direct answer to the question and forget that you must also say *why* you have made this choice. Though the *weak* response does supply a reason, it is fairly shallow, and the candidate misses the opportunity to discuss a personal trait with the interviewer. To make the most of this opportunity, pick the object that has some link to a skill or trait you really do have. In the *strong* response, the candidate highlighted their resilience by picking the liver, but you can choose any skill and find an organ that matches that skill. If you want to highlight your extroversion, you might choose the heart, which pumps blood to the rest of the body. If you are a good communicator and leader, you might choose the brain, which directs signals to the rest of the body to ensure proper functioning. Once you have made and justified your choice, provide some supporting evidence to show that you have the skill or trait you identified, and, if appropriate, discuss how you could apply it in the future.

Question 13: What makes you angry?

Weak response:

I don't really get angry about too much (**dismisses the emotion**). I think one thing that makes me angry is when people are late. That annoys me because I have waited for someone to show up to something and they did not respect my time or effort (**answer does not give example and is focused on something that affects the self**).

Strong response:

This is an interesting question. After reflecting, one thing that makes me angry is seeing a lack of medical resources, especially in regard to patient care (**identifies something that affects others, not just the self, showing empathy**). For example, at the local hospital where I volunteer, patients are often told they need certain medications that their insurance does not cover and most of them cannot afford these medications out-of-pocket. This makes me angry because I would like to see these patients get the best possible care and a lack of resources should not affect their health outcomes (**clearly gives example and says why it makes them angry**). I would love to work to alleviate this problem as a physician. As a volunteer, I have been able to assist patients in calling their insurance companies, but as a physician, I will be able to advocate for far better resources and minimize health-care inequities (**suggests a proactive way forward**).

Discussion:

Medical school interviews can and will ask you to talk about negative emotions and experiences, not just positive ones. It is critical that you not sidestep this question, but rather be honest and vulnerable with your response. In the *weak* response, the candidate first downplays the emotion, then identifies a source of anger that is self-focused. If you have many emotions, experiences, or issues to choose from, focus on one that is motivated by injustice for vulnerable parties beyond yourself, such as patients, students, and marginalized individuals. As always, a *strong* answer like the one above not only gives appropriate details from an observation or interaction that illustrates the point, it should also include a discussion on how the candidate moved past the event or acted to solve the problem, as well as the overarching lessons learned and how these might impact their future. These are challenging questions, so take time to reflect on which experiences you can use to demonstrate your maturity and professionalism.

Question 14: Teach me something in the next 2 minutes.

Weak response:

I don't really have anything I can teach, sorry. I don't have any interesting skills (**panic reaction**). Um, I guess I can teach you how to hit a forehand, since I play tennis. OK, so you would hold your hand out to the side like this and swing this way (the candidate would swing their arm). Can you repeat that? (**no clarification, no stepwise approach, does not solicit feedback**).

Strong response:

I would like to teach you to how to say a few words in Hindi, if that is alright with you (**identifies the task clearly**). If I am not clear about anything, please let me know (**asks for feedback proactively**). I am going to teach you how to count to three and we will be repeating each word before stringing them together. The Hindi word for *one* is "ek". Can you repeat it for me? Great! The word for *two* is "do". Can I hear you try it? The word for *three* is "teen". Same thing, I would love to hear you say it back to me. Thank you. Now, let's put it together: "ek, do, teen" (**step-by-step instructions**). Great, it sounds like you have it! And that's how you say *one, two, three* in Hindi. Do you have any questions or feedback for me (**asks for feedback at the end**)?

Discussion:

This is a tricky question, one that our students struggle with occasionally during our preparation programs. Candidates often think they have nothing to teach the interviewers, get flustered, and fumble at the beginning of their answer before giving rushed, unclear instructions on how to do a task, as exemplified in the *weak* response. Remember, what you teach does not have to be a complicated skill, just something simple but unique. Think hard about your background, extracurricular activities, and interests. Do you play a sport, speak another language, play an instrument, or have a hobby? What is a basic part of that activity that you could easily teach someone of any age in three steps? Once you have settled on what you will teach, you must think of this as a collaborative task. As the candidate does in the *strong* response, prepare the interviewer by telling them what you are about to teach them. Then, guide them by giving clear, step-by-step instructions and checking in regularly to ensure they are keeping up with you. This way, you are teaching them something *and* using your communication skills to keep them engaged.

Question 15: Define patient-centred care.

Weak response:

Patient-centred care is very important. I believe it means you must listen to the patient and aim to meet their desires and goals, not just your own goals as the physician (**defines the term**). This is something I have come to appreciate during my volunteering role in the hospital (**gives no further details or examples**). I believe patient-centred care is key to being a great physician (**does not identify *why* this is important for physicians**).

Strong response:

Thank you for asking this question. I have seen that your school highly values patient-centred care (**knowledge about the school or program's mission statement and values**). To me, patient-centred care means identifying the patient's perspective and taking that into consideration when making a treatment plan (**succinct definition**). For example, when I shadowed Dr. Smith in his primary-care clinic, I saw him interact with one patient who smoked. Dr. Smith recommended cutting back on the number of cigarettes this patient was smoking every day as a stepwise approach to quitting smoking. However, Dr. Smith took the time to ask this patient what his barriers to quitting or cutting back were. The patient identified that smoking was a stress relief for him. He was a low-income hourly wage worker and also going through a stressful time at home with his girlfriend. Smoking was a quick way for him to relax and he was hesitant to stop. Dr. Smith listened, empathized with the patient, and gave him other resources for tackling stress, as well as information about affordable treatments to start cutting back on smoking (**thorough yet concise example showing the definition of patient-centred care**). What I learned from this was that you must identify the patient's goals and barriers to accessing the treatments you suggest. As I move forward in my education, I must not only offer evidence-based treatments, but follow Dr. Smith's example of taking the time to explore the patient's perspective. This will help me practice patient-centered care (**highlights learning outcome and future application**).

Discussion:

At your medical school interview, you may be asked to discuss or define abstract concepts, which may come in the form of a single term, as in the question above, or even as a quote. After you have defined the concept, follow the strategy for answering personal questions in the remainder of your response. In the *weak* answer, the candidate gives a quick definition of the quote without highlighting examples or learning outcomes. In the *strong* answer, the candidate states what the term means to them personally, then gives a clear example *showing* how the definition applies in practice, then highlights the learning outcome and application of this concept in the future. Giving an example and telling the interviewer what you learned goes a long way in showing that you have the maturity to reflect on and grow from your experiences so that you are continuously building on the values and tools that will make you a successful physician.

Question 16: What are your career goals?

Weak response:

I am certain that I want to go into cardiology. I have an interest in the cardiovascular system and I have done significant research in that subfield with Dr. Miller at my university. As soon as I get into medical school, I am looking to expand my knowledge of this area so I can work towards matching to cardiology in the future (**very definite path, not open to learning or changing**).

Strong response:

This is a very important question to consider. Right now, I am focused on getting into medical school, but with the experiences I have had so far, I am considering practicing primary care. I have shadowed multiple primary care physicians in my city and have enjoyed the continuity of care and long-term patient interactions, as well as the broad approach those physicians take (**identifies an area they enjoy and states why**). However, at this stage, I am open to learning more about the other fields in medicine as well. I would like to take the time to explore different specialties and find one that I am a good fit for and can contribute to (**shows openness to exploration, learning, and changing**). I would also like teaching to be a part of my future career, regardless of the specialty I go into. I have learned so much from the doctors I have shadowed that I want to be able to give back to future learners in the same way (**highlights non-clinical roles to be involved in**).

Discussion:

Many medical school interviewers will want to know what your future goals are. Candidates, like the one who gave the *weak* response, often think that they must have a definite answer here and show dedication to one path. However, it is common for medical students to change their minds about their desired specialty several times during medical school, so interviewers never expect you to have a definite plan prior to beginning your studies. They, instead, expect you to identify the aspects of medicine you are interested in and why. The *strong* answer above does specify a particular area, but more importantly, the candidate explains why they liked that particular specialty and also indicates that they are open and even eager to explore other options. The candidate also highlights the teaching aspect of medicine that they hope to engage in regardless of their future specialty. Other such aspects for you to consider include research, administrative work, rural vs. urban practice, inpatient vs. outpatient setting, and so forth. With such a response, you demonstrate your knowledge about the medical profession, as well as your respect for all the fields of medicine. Openness and flexibility are key qualities for a medical student, and you must display that in your answer.

Question 17: Consider the following scenario. You are a primary care physician and you must tell your 75-year-old patient, Mr. Smith, to cease driving as it is no longer safe for him to do so. How would you approach Mr. Smith?

Weak response:

I would tell Mr. Smith that, due to his age and other factors, it is no longer safe for him to drive as this would pose a danger to him and others. He may be resistant to this piece of information, so I'd have to let him know that I would have to report him if he continued driving (**judgmental, does not acknowledge the patient's needs**).

Strong response:

In this situation, I am a primary care physician who is talking to a senior patient of mine about his ability to drive (**presents a brief recap**). My main concern here is for the well-being of my patient, Mr. Smith, and the well-being of others on the road (**identifies the pressing issue and vulnerable parties**). I would begin by having Mr. Smith come into my office and ask him if he knows why I have asked him to come for the appointment. I would then directly but empathetically let him know that he should no longer be driving, highlighting my concern for his safety and the safety of others. I would then ask Mr. Smith how much he drives and for what purposes because it is important that I take the time to explore the impact this would make on his life and to find alternative solutions for him (**gathers information**). I would look into resources to help him get around town without driving and ask him if he has any questions. It's quite possible he would be upset at this news. If that's the case, I would ask him to share his concerns with me and work to address them. While I do need to be firm about the recommendation, I also want to compassionately reiterate my concern for his safety and assure him that I will do everything I can to help him minimize the impact this will have on his day-to-day activities. (**directly states facts but takes patient's well-being and perspective into consideration, offers concrete solutions**). I would then suggest we meet for a follow-up appointment in about a week's time so I can check in with him and ensure he is able to access the resources he needs (**proactive follow-up**). If I found out he were not adhering to my suggestions, I would have to let him know that, again for his safety and that of others, I would have to report him (**considers worst-case hypothetical**). In summary, I would keep Mr. Smith's and the public's well-being at the forefront of my mind while working with my patient to make a well-thought-out plan for the future (**summarizes briefly**).

Discussion:

This is a scenario-type question once again, so we would encourage you to follow the suggested strategies, which include briefly recapping the scenario, identifying the pressing issue, gathering information, outlining 2 to 3 hypothetical situations and solutions, and summarizing your approach. In the *weak* response, the candidate lacks compassion, showing no concern for how this change will negatively impact the patient's life. In the *strong* response, the candidate identifies the pressing issue as the well-being of the patient and others on the road and relays the information with empathy. The candidate then takes time to gather information about the patient's particular concerns and needs, then proposes a plan to help him reduce the negative impact this reduced mobility will have. Finally, the candidate plans to follow up with the patient to ensure that he is following the recommendations and to monitor his adjustment. The brief recap and summary ensure that the answer is organized and coherent. Approaching scenario-type questions with this strategy will guarantee that your answer is both in-depth and concise.

Question 18: What is one solution you would suggest to alleviate the shortage of physicians in rural areas?

Weak response:

One solution that can be implemented here is to make medical students work in a rural area for 5 years after their training is completed. This will ensure rural areas do have enough physicians to serve the patients in those areas (**suggests a solution but answer lacks depth**).

Strong response:

I am aware that this is a topic that is getting more and more coverage as the shortage of practitioners in rural areas becomes a problem for everyone. Shortage of health care practitioners may cause disproportionate health impacts to populations in rural areas, so it's imperative that the medical profession work to solve this issue (**demonstrates awareness of topic**). One solution I can think of is trying to recruit more medical students from rural areas (**identifies one solution**). There are pros and cons to this solution. A possible pro is that students already from rural areas have family and friends there and are most likely to go back and begin serving those communities after completing their training. On the other hand, it could be unfair to those students who are not from rural areas but are genuinely interested in practicing there. Since this could affect the admissions screening process, it could screen out those from urban areas who want to practice rurally (**discussion of pros and cons of this solution**). In my opinion, this type of screening measure would work best if, rather than preferentially choosing students from rural areas, medical schools find out which students are genuinely interested in practicing in rural areas, whether they are from an urban or a rural setting. They can, for example, select students who have had positive experiences working with rural or marginalized populations. I feel this type of solution will be best to find future physicians who wish to practice in rural areas, while still being fair to all medical students (**gives opinion and suggests an alternative solution**).

Discussion:

You may have identified this as a policy question. In the *weak* response, the candidate offers a solution without discussing it in-depth. To give a more thorough answer, use the approach we suggested for policy questions. This is exemplified in the *strong* answer, where the candidate shows an awareness of this hot topic and identifies a possible solution for which they briefly discuss both pros and cons. The candidate then gives their own opinion and suggests an alternative that would work better. Following this strategy will ensure that your answer is in-depth and balanced, and that your own stance is presented clearly and backed by well-reasoned points. As the question stem specifies, only one possible solution is discussed. Though you may feel the need to name multiple solutions, pay attention to the question and only give as many solutions as asked for! This shows your attention to detail.

Question 19: What would you change about this program?

Weak response:

This program is wonderful in every way. I cannot identify anything I would change (**avoids answering the question**).

Strong response:

Thank you asking me this question. I appreciate the opportunity to share my opinion. I have learned a lot about your program through your website and by speaking with other students at today's interview, and I truly believe it's a wonderful program (**highlights research into the program**). One area I feel passionate about is student wellness (**identifies an area of interest**). At my university, I co-founded and continue to run a peer support listening program, which allows students to anonymously call in and receive support from trained peer volunteers. Students who have used this program have reported that speaking with one of our volunteers has helped greatly with stress management (**outlines proactive approach to contribute to this area**). Medical school is difficult and stressful, and students often need support from colleagues and teachers. I have seen that your program has really worked hard to promote wellness by having various programs like game nights and discussion groups, but I have not seen a peer listening group listed as a resource. I would love to be able to start something like this at your program if I am fortunate enough to begin medical school here (**suggests an additional program that could be added and takes a proactive approach to starting it**).

Discussion:

This is a tricky question! In the *weak* answer, the candidate likely avoids answering due to fear of offending the interviewers. This is the wrong attitude to have because no school is perfect. Interviewers want to see that you have taken the time to fully research their program, therefore showing genuine interest, and that you have ideas about how to change their program for the better. The candidate who gives the *strong* answer does precisely this. They begin by outlining the avenues through which they have learned about the program and picks one particular area they feel passionate about and have experience with. The candidate then identifies a beneficial program the school is lacking, and most importantly, takes on the responsibility of starting the program themselves. To answer this question well, you must have done enough homework on the program beforehand. You can then suggest an alternative or improvement that you yourself can contribute to. This shows the school you will take an active role in contributing to the betterment of their program and community.

Question 20. What is your approach to leadership?

Weak response:

I think leadership is important and I work every day to gain more leadership skills. I like to ensure I listen to others and take their perspectives into account, rather than simply stating my opinion and implementing my solutions (**no backing evidence given**). My leadership role as captain of the basketball team has prepared me to take on more leadership roles in the future (**introduces source of leadership skills but does not give specific examples or learning outcomes**).

Strong response:

Leadership is a very important aspect of being a professional, especially a physician. My approach to leadership has been shaped by my roles as a co-founder of the neuroscience club on campus, as a volunteer coordinator, and as captain of my intramural floor hockey team (**identifies important leadership roles held**). I would like to speak about one example that I learned from most. As captain of my intramural team, I am responsible for scheduling game times. Last semester, some of my teammates wanted all the games to be scheduled on weekends so they could have weekdays to study, while other group members wanted some games to be on weekdays so they could go home on weekends to visit family. As team captain, the decision was mine to make, but I talked with each team member individually first to get their opinions without any influence from others. I then called a team meeting where I encouraged everyone to share their opinions and propose solutions. We had a very productive discussion, and the solution we ultimately decided on was to have a rotating schedule and rotating roster, where we played some games on weekends and some on weekdays, and different players played depending on the day the game was (**gives example clearly showing actions taken**). I learned a lot about leadership from this experience. I learned that I must not jump to conclusions and that I must allow everyone to contribute and collaborate on a solution. I also learned that decisive action should only follow empathetic information gathering. People look up to physicians as leaders in their communities and I will keep these lessons in mind moving forward (**learning outcomes and future application highlighted**).

Discussion:

This personal question asks about an important skill that physicians must have. Though the question does not ask for it directly, you must give an example of how you demonstrate the skill, using the structure for personal-type questions to guide you. Though the candidate who gives the *weak* response does describe how and where they demonstrate leadership, no examples are given to back their claims. On the other hand, the candidate who gives the *strong* answer identifies three important leadership roles they have held and focuses on a specific example from one of these roles to show how they used their leadership skills. Importantly, the candidate outlines the learning outcomes and why these skills are important for physicians to have. To effectively answer these personal type questions, take the time now to reflect on your experiences and prepare personal examples that you can use during your medical school interview.

Now that you have had the time to try out these sample questions and read through our example responses and expert discussions, you should be getting comfortable with the strategies for each question type. In the next chapter, you will have further opportunities to practice what you know with 100 more questions. Before you begin, make sure you can identify the different question types and outline the correct approach to each. We will give you further instructions in the next chapter.

Happy practicing!

CHAPTER XIII

100 Practice Medical School Interview Questions

Now that you have familiarized yourself with the strategies for answering different types of questions and seen sample questions and expert responses, you can put your knowledge to the test! This chapter provides 10 independent sets of interview question sets for you to practice.

Each set contains 10 questions, including variants of the three most frequently asked panel questions ("Tell us about yourself", "Why medicine?", and "Why our program?"), as well as scenario, policy, personal, and quirky questions. Before you respond to a question, make sure you have identified the question type, then proceed using the appropriate structure. This will ensure that your answers are organized and comprehensive. If you need to review the question types and structures, please revisit *Chapter VII: Proven Strategies to Approach and Ace Any Medical School Interview Question*.

For the first few questions, write out an outline of your responses before practicing out loud. This will help you to be more confident with your use of the strategies. Later on, to make your practice more realistic, consider having a friend pose the questions to you as the interviewer. We also recommend that you begin recording your responses so that you can review them afterwards. This will enable you to track the length of your answers, your delivery, areas that need to be more concise, areas that need to be expanded or supplemented, red flags, and of course, your overall progress. To complete your practice, be sure to get objective, expert feedback either from a mature professional or by signing up for a BeMo preparation program. The expert will be able to point out areas in need of improvement that you missed and keep you on track as you work toward your goals.

A caveat: As you become familiar with the strategies and transitions, and get comfortable with certain personal examples, you may find that some of your answers begin to sound similar, or that you are using the same examples again and again. If this happens, it would be a good idea to take a step back and reflect on what other traits, interests, or experiences you could discuss to diversify your answers. Create a bank of these ideas that you can draw from with discretion and flexibility. Remember, it is very rare to encounter the *exact* same question twice. As you will see, even the three most frequently asked panel questions will be framed differently each time. Therefore, it is normal and often necessary for the content of your answer to change as well. What should remain consistent each time is the structure, organization, and flow of your response, and the relevance of your points to the question.

Are you ready? Let's begin!

Interview Set 1

Question 1

When did you decide that medicine is for you? What have you done since to confirm that decision?

What type of question is this?

What's the most pressing issue?

What is the best strategy?

Question 2

What are the three things about our program or curriculum that excites you most?

<u>What type of question is this?</u>

<u>What's the most pressing issue?</u>

<u>What is the best strategy?</u>

Question 3

Can you tell the panel about yourself?

What type of question is this?

What's the most pressing issue?

What is the best strategy?

Question 4

In what ways is the healthcare system in the U.S./Canada not representative of the population it serves? As a future physician, how will you promote inclusion, equity, and diversity in your profession?

What type of question is this?

What's the most pressing issue?

What is the best strategy?

Question 5

Consider the following scenario: You have a terminally ill patient who wants to see his daughter get married before he dies. The therapy that is sustaining his life is extremely expensive and already putting a huge financial burden on the patient's family. What would you do in this case?

What type of question is this?

What theme(s) can you identify?

What's the most pressing issue?

What are the missing facts?

Who is directly and indirectly involved?

What are some hypothetical situations and solutions? Frame using the *if/then* structure.

Question 6

Governments have responded to the global COVID-19 outbreak differently. Some have been more effective at containing the spread of the virus than others. Discuss what methods and policies you think are effective and which are not in the face of an outbreak like this.

<u>What type of question is this?</u>

<u>What's the most pressing issue?</u>

<u>What is the best strategy?</u>

Question 7

Consider the following scenario: You use your account and credit card to book an Airbnb for your visiting relatives. Shortly after they check out and leave, the Airbnb host contacts you to notify you that some of the items from the room you booked went missing. They will be charging you for these items and this incident will negatively affect your Airbnb rating. What would you do in this situation?

What type of question is this?

What theme(s) can you identify?

What's the most pressing issue?

What are the missing facts?

Who is directly and indirectly involved?

What are some hypothetical situations and solutions? Frame using the *if/then* structure.

Question 8

What is the most difficult conversation you've had with a family member?

What type of question is this?

What's the most pressing issue?

What is the best strategy?

Question 9

When you are feeling unmotivated, who or what do you turn to for inspiration?

What type of question is this?

What's the most pressing issue?

What is the best strategy?

Question 10

What season of the year do you relate to the most? Why?

What type of question is this?

What's the most pressing issue?

What is the best strategy?

Interview Set 2

Question 1

What are the three most essential things to know about you?

What type of question is this?

What's the most pressing issue?

What is the best strategy?

Question 2

Who are your role models? How did they influence your decision to pursue medicine?

What type of question is this?

What's the most pressing issue?

What is the best strategy?

Question 3

Why did you select [school: ___________________]? How do you see yourself contributing to our program?

<u>What type of question is this?</u>

<u>What's the most pressing issue?</u>

<u>What is the best strategy?</u>

Question 4

Consider the following scenario: Your neighbor Betty, a single mom, entrusts you with babysitting her two grade school kids on weekday evenings from 6-11pm while she works a late-night shift. You're one of the few people who gets along with her kids, and the extra income is also helping with your ever-increasing rent. Come the new school semester, the director of your jazz band tells you that your rehearsal time has been changed to 6-8pm on Tuesdays and Thursdays because that's the only time that doesn't conflict with everyone's class schedules. What would you do in this situation?

What type of question is this?

What theme(s) can you identify?

What's the most pressing issue?

What are the missing facts?

Who is directly and indirectly involved?

What are some hypothetical situations and solutions? Frame using the *if/then* structure.

Question 5

The media is an important source of information, but it has also been heavily criticized for its biased coverage of certain issues. What is one global issue that you feel has not received enough media coverage?

What type of question is this?

What's the most pressing issue?

What is the best strategy?

Question 6

In what ways is the climate crisis going to impact your local healthcare system?

What type of question is this?

What's the most pressing issue?

What is the best strategy?

Question 7

Consider the following scenario: You are the primary care physician to an elderly patient who is terminally ill. Her family asks you not to tell her the truth about her condition, but your patient asks that you be honest with her. The family comes from a culture where doctors do not reveal this kind of news to senior patients even when they ask. What would you do?

<u>What type of question is this?</u>

<u>What theme(s) can you identify?</u>

<u>What's the most pressing issue?</u>

What are the missing facts?

Who is directly and indirectly involved?

What are some hypothetical situations and solutions? Frame using the *if/then* structure.

Question 8

What would be the hardest thing for you to let go of right now?

What type of question is this?

What's the most pressing issue?

What is the best strategy?

Question 9

Tell us about a time when your actions had a negative impact on someone else.

What type of question is this?

What's the most pressing issue?

What is the best strategy?

Question 10

Given the chance, what extreme sport would you try (next)?

What type of question is this?

What's the most pressing issue?

What is the best strategy?

Interview Set 3

Question 1

Why have you chosen to pursue medicine and not another related profession such as nursing, pharmacy, or dentistry?

What type of question is this?

What's the most pressing issue?

What is the best strategy?

Question 2

Tell the panel about who you are in a few short points.

What type of question is this?

What's the most pressing issue?

What is the best strategy?

Question 3

What do you think are the strengths of our program that sets us apart from other programs?

What type of question is this?

What's the most pressing issue?

What is the best strategy?

Question 4

Consider the following scenario: You and 5 other friends rent a cottage for a summer get-away. The night before the trip, one of them, your best friend, informs you that he will no longer be able to make the trip for a reason he doesn't want you to share with the others. You are understanding of the situation, but the other friends are furious and demand that he pays his share of the costs. What would you do in this situation?

What type of question is this?

What theme(s) can you identify?

What's the most pressing issue?

What are the missing facts?

Who is directly and indirectly involved?

What are some hypothetical situations and solutions? Frame using the *if/then* structure.

Question 5

If you could start a non-profit organization, which current global issue would you tackle? Briefly outline the specific things your organization would do to resolve/alleviate the issue.

What type of question is this?

What's the most pressing issue?

What is the best strategy?

Question 6

What is one underserved population in your community? How would you advocate for them as a physician?

<u>What type of question is this?</u>

<u>What's the most pressing issue?</u>

<u>What is the best strategy?</u>

Question 7

Consider the following scenario: You are interviewing for a residency position at your hospital of choice. Your best friend gets the position and you don't. You later find out that her uncle works in that very department. What would you do?

What type of question is this?

What theme(s) can you identify?

What's the most pressing issue?

What are the missing facts?

Who is directly and indirectly involved?

What are some hypothetical situations and solutions? Frame using the *if/then* structure.

Question 8

Tell us about a time when your beliefs were challenged.

What type of question is this?

What's the most pressing issue?

What is the best strategy?

Question 9

What empowers you to break through the barriers you face in life?

What type of question is this?

What's the most pressing issue?

What is the best strategy?

Question 10

What was the most enjoyable meal you've had recently? Why?

What type of question is this?

What's the most pressing issue?

What is the best strategy?

Interview Set 4

Question 1

Briefly tell the panel about yourself, your interests, and what makes you unique.

What type of question is this?

What's the most pressing issue?

What is the best strategy?

Question 2

What made you decide on a career in medicine?

What type of question is this?

What's the most pressing issue?

What is the best strategy?

Question 3

Knowing that you wanted to pursue this profession, why did you decide to apply to our program?

What type of question is this?

What's the most pressing issue?

What is the best strategy?

Question 4

Consider the following scenario: Your family is not well-off, and you've had to work part-time throughout college to pay for your own tuition. The year you're set to graduate, your family asks you to take a semester off school to work and help pay for your younger sister's first year tuition the coming fall. What would you do in this situation?

What type of question is this?

What theme(s) can you identify?

What's the most pressing issue?

What are the missing facts?

Who is directly and indirectly involved?

What are some hypothetical situations and solutions? Frame using the *if/then* structure.

Question 5

Insulin is ten times more expensive in some countries than others. What are your thoughts on this issue?

What type of question is this?

What's the most pressing issue?

What is the best strategy?

Question 6

What is the role of the physician in providing medical aid to other countries and promoting global health?

What type of question is this?

What's the most pressing issue?

What is the best strategy?

Question 7

Have you ever been discouraged by someone else? What did you do in response?

What type of question is this?

What's the most pressing issue?

What is the best strategy?

Question 8

Consider the following scenario: You are the primary care physician to a young female patient who has come into your office to ask for an early abortion. This goes against your personal values and beliefs. What would you do?

What type of question is this?

What theme(s) can you identify?

What's the most pressing issue?

What are the missing facts?

Who is directly and indirectly involved?

What are some hypothetical situations and solutions? Frame using the *if/then* structure.

Question 9

Complete this sentence: I feel most like myself when ________. Explain your answer.

What type of question is this?

What's the most pressing issue?

What is the best strategy?

Question 10

If you could take one person with you to travel around the world, who would it be?

What type of question is this?

What's the most pressing issue?

What is the best strategy?

Interview Set 5

Question 1

Briefly describe three of your favorite activities, using them to tell the panel about who you are as a person.

What type of question is this?

What's the most pressing issue?

What is the best strategy?

Question 2

What are the top three reasons you want to pursue medicine?

What type of question is this?

What's the most pressing issue?

What is the best strategy?

Question 3

In what ways did our program stand out to you when you were selecting schools?

What type of question is this?

What's the most pressing issue?

What is the best strategy?

Question 4

Consider the following scenario: You are on the bus and running late for work because of bad weather and traffic. You get off the phone with your manager who is upset and threatening to lay you off if you don't get there within the next half hour. At this time, you overhear an elderly passenger struggle to communicate with the bus driver using broken English. She seems lost and confused about where she's supposed to get off. You recognize her accent and realize you speak the same language, so you get up to help her translate. She is exceedingly grateful and asks if you can help take her home. What would you do in this situation?

What type of question is this?

What theme(s) can you identify?

What's the most pressing issue?

What are the missing facts?

Who is directly and indirectly involved?

What are some hypothetical situations and solutions? Frame using the *if/then* structure.

Question 5

What are your views on minors making decisions on their own health care treatments and giving consent?

What type of question is this?

What's the most pressing issue?

What is the best strategy?

Question 6

What is the ideal working relationship between healthcare professionals and the government to ensure that health policies are maximally beneficial to the population they serve?

What type of question is this?

What's the most pressing issue?

What is the best strategy?

Question 7

Tell us about a time when you had a lapse in judgment.

<u>What type of question is this?</u>

<u>What's the most pressing issue?</u>

<u>What is the best strategy?</u>

Question 8

Consider the following scenario: You are a psychiatrist. One of your patients, who is a single mother, often brings her son and has him wait outside while you conduct your sessions with her. One day as they're leaving, you notice bruises on the child's neck and arms. What would you do in this situation?

<u>What type of question is this?</u>

<u>What theme(s) can you identify?</u>

<u>What's the most pressing issue?</u>

<u>What are the missing facts?</u>

Who is directly and indirectly involved?

What are some hypothetical situations and solutions? Frame using the *if/then* structure.

Question 9

Who do you want to get to know better in your life? Why?

What type of question is this?

What's the most pressing issue?

What is the best strategy?

Question 10

What is one thing you cannot travel without?

What type of question is this?

What's the most pressing issue?

What is the best strategy?

Interview Set 6

Question 1

Tell us something that is unique about you.

What type of question is this?

What's the most pressing issue?

What is the best strategy?

Question 2

How will you contribute to our program's mission, which is focused on diversity and research?

What type of question is this?

What's the most pressing issue?

What is the best strategy?

Question 3

Could you briefly speak about your journey to medicine?

<u>What type of question is this?</u>

<u>What's the most pressing issue?</u>

<u>What is the best strategy?</u>

Question 4

Could you tell us about a time you failed to stand up for something that was particularly important to you?

What type of question is this?

What's the most pressing issue?

What is the best strategy?

Question 5

Consider the following scenario: Your good friend shares with you that his partner is involved in some potentially illegal activity. He is too scared to approach his partner, but also wants to ensure their safety. He turns to you for advice. What would you tell your friend?

<u>What type of question is this?</u>

<u>What theme(s) can you identify?</u>

<u>What's the most pressing issue?</u>

<u>What are the missing facts?</u>

Who is directly and indirectly involved?

What are some hypothetical situations and solutions? Frame using the *if/then* structure.

Question 6

The World Health Organization (WHO) has declared a new pandemic, and state governments have responded by prohibiting individuals from working and requiring them to stay inside their homes for a period of time. What are some benefits and drawbacks to these restrictions?

What type of question is this?

What's the most pressing issue?

What is the best strategy?

Question 7

Consider the following scenario: You are a newly hired assistant in a busy clinic working for a notable doctor who is fully booked for the next few months. A distressed mother walks in with her child. She is a newer patient at the clinic but does not have an appointment for that day. What would you do?

What type of question is this?

What theme(s) can you identify?

What's the most pressing issue?

What are the missing facts?

Who is directly and indirectly involved?

What are some hypothetical situations and solutions? Frame using the *if/then* structure.

Question 8

Imagine a 6-year-old child asks you to help them tie their shoelaces. How would you go about teaching them? Could you walk us through the steps?

<u>What type of question is this?</u>

<u>What's the most pressing issue?</u>

<u>What is the best strategy?</u>

Question 9

What are two unique health challenges faced by indigenous communities today? What can the government do to improve their conditions?

What type of question is this?

What's the most pressing issue?

What is the best strategy?

Question 10

What's an area that you feel needs improvement but have delayed working on? Why?

What type of question is this?

What's the most pressing issue?

What is the best strategy?

Interview Set 7

Question 1

If you were to receive an award for something notable you've done, what would it be for?

What type of question is this?

What's the most pressing issue?

What is the best strategy?

Question 2

Why are you specifically interested in this program and not others?

What type of question is this?

What's the most pressing issue?

What is the best strategy?

Question 3

There are many other ways to improve local and global health. Why did you specifically choose to pursue medicine?

What type of question is this?

What's the most pressing issue?

What is the best strategy?

Question 4

Is there anything you would change about our program?

What type of question is this?

What's the most pressing issue?

What is the best strategy?

Question 5

Can you tell us about an experience that involved poor decision-making on your part? What was the result? What have you learned from this?

What type of question is this?

What's the most pressing issue?

What is the best strategy?

Question 6

Consider the following scenario: You are a 3rd year student and are approached by your professor in class who asks if you can lead the discussion for him as he needs to step out for a few minutes. You happily oblige. 20 minutes later, the professor returns smelling of alcohol. What would you do?

<u>What type of question is this?</u>

<u>What theme(s) can you identify?</u>

<u>What's the most pressing issue?</u>

<u>What are the missing facts?</u>

Who is directly and indirectly involved?

What are some hypothetical situations and solutions? Frame using the *if/then* structure.

Question 7

A new hospital policy mandates all physicians to make themselves available to patients outside of their working hours through mobile services. What are your thoughts on this?

What type of question is this?

What's the most pressing issue?

What is the best strategy?

Question 8

If you had the resources to help any developing country, which one would it be? Why?

What type of question is this?

What's the most pressing issue?

What is the best strategy?

Question 9

In your opinion, what are two changes that need to be made to ensure effective patient care in your community?

What type of question is this?

What's the most pressing issue?

What is the best strategy?

Question 10

If you were the interviewer, what is one question you think is necessary to ask all medical school applicants?

<u>What type of question is this?</u>

<u>What's the most pressing issue?</u>

<u>What is the best strategy?</u>

Interview Set 8

Question 1

What are your motivations for pursuing medicine? What makes you an ideal doctor?

What type of question is this?

What's the most pressing issue?

What is the best strategy?

Question 2

If we were to ask your closest friends to tell us about you, what are 3 things they might say?

<u>What type of question is this?</u>

<u>What's the most pressing issue?</u>

<u>What is the best strategy?</u>

Question 3

Consider the following scenario: You recently graduated university and are interviewing for a summer research position. The supervisor interviewing you openly tells you after your interview that he likes you, but due to recent structural changes they do not have the budget in their project funds. However, they could pay you some cash, and work out a system if you would like. How would you respond?

What type of question is this?

What theme(s) can you identify?

What's the most pressing issue?

What are the missing facts?

Who is directly and indirectly involved?

What are some hypothetical situations and solutions? Frame using the *if/then* structure.

Question 4

Discuss an embarrassing moment you experienced recently. Why was it embarrassing?

What type of question is this?

What's the most pressing issue?

What is the best strategy?

Question 5

Our program prides itself in having a diverse student body. In what ways would you contribute to this diversity?

What type of question is this?

What's the most pressing issue?

What is the best strategy?

Question 6

What would you change about the medical school admissions process?

What type of question is this?

What's the most pressing issue?

What is the best strategy?

Question 7

If you could take part in any current stream of research, which would it be and why?

<u>What type of question is this?</u>

<u>What's the most pressing issue?</u>

<u>What is the best strategy?</u>

Question 8

Can you tell us about an experience that made you grateful?

What type of question is this?

What's the most pressing issue?

What is the best strategy?

Question 9

What are your thoughts on policies that require International Medical Graduates (IMGs) to undergo more training than what is required of non-IMG students?

What type of question is this?

What's the most pressing issue?

What is the best strategy?

Question 10

Consider the following scenario: You are an elementary school teacher. During parent-teacher night, a parent of one of your students comes into your office very upset about the report card their child received, blaming you for their child's poor academic performance. What would you do in this case?

What type of question is this?

What theme(s) can you identify?

What's the most pressing issue?

What are the missing facts?

Who is directly and indirectly involved?

What are some hypothetical situations and solutions? Frame using the *if/then* structure.

Interview Set 9

Question 1

When did you decide to become a doctor and what kinds of activities have you participated in since to prepare you for the profession?

What type of question is this?

What's the most pressing issue?

What is the best strategy?

Question 2

Should physicians be able to refuse to give certain treatments to patients if that kind of treatment is legal but goes against their religious beliefs? What are your thoughts?

What type of question is this?

What's the most pressing issue?

What is the best strategy?

Question 3

Tell the panel about yourself, specifically, what you value most and why.

What type of question is this?

What's the most pressing issue?

What is the best strategy?

Question 4

What is one thing you hope to gain from our program and one thing you see yourself contributing?

What type of question is this?

What's the most pressing issue?

What is the best strategy?

Question 5

Consider the following scenario: You are on a production team filming a television show. Since it's your first project, you put in a lot of work and extra hours, and often take on other people's responsibilities as well. When the show finally airs, you see that your name has been left out of the credits. What would you do?

What type of question is this?

What theme(s) can you identify?

What's the most pressing issue?

What are the missing facts?

Who is directly and indirectly involved?

What are some hypothetical situations and solutions? Frame using the *if/then* structure.

Question 6

What are your thoughts on e-cigarettes and vaping?

What type of question is this?

What's the most pressing issue?

What is the best strategy?

Question 7

Have you ever been disappointed by one of the people you look up to? What was your response?

What type of question is this?

What's the most pressing issue?

What is the best strategy?

Question 8

Consider the following scenario: On your early morning run, you see a group of teenagers in an alleyway. As you get closer, they walk away, and you see a homeless person huddled in the corner. You notice that he's shaking, and he has some bruises on his face. What would you do?

<u>What type of question is this?</u>

<u>What theme(s) can you identify?</u>

<u>What's the most pressing issue?</u>

<u>What are the missing facts?</u>

Who is directly and indirectly involved?

What are some hypothetical situations and solutions? Frame using the *if/then* structure.

Question 9

If you could be any instrument, which would you be and why?

What type of question is this?

What's the most pressing issue?

What is the best strategy?

Question 10

What do you think will be most challenging for you in your future career? Why?

What type of question is this?

What's the most pressing issue?

What is the best strategy?

Interview Set 10

Question 1

What are three words that best describe you? Why did you pick these words?

What type of question is this?

What's the most pressing issue?

What is the best strategy?

Question 2

Consider the following scenario: You are a mailman. As you are dropping off someone's mail at their house, you hear shouting and the sound of someone crying from beyond the door. There is no one else around and the neighborhood is not considered safe. What would you do?

What type of question is this?

What theme(s) can you identify?

What's the most pressing issue?

What are the missing facts?

Who is directly and indirectly involved?

What are some hypothetical situations and solutions? Frame using the *if/then* structure.

Question 3

What do you look forward to most about your future career that isn't offered by any other line of work?

What type of question is this?

What's the most pressing issue?

What is the best strategy?

Question 4

Do you think minors should be allowed to make decisions about their treatment? If yes, under what circumstances?

What type of question is this?

What's the most pressing issue?

What is the best strategy?

Question 5

Consider the following scenario: You are a graduate student researcher who supervises the work of some undergraduate research assistants for your advisor. When it comes time to report the progress of their work, you realize that a large portion of the data was not included in the analysis as you had instructed and the analysis itself is problematic. There is no time to amend these errors before your meeting. What would you do?

<u>What type of question is this?</u>

<u>What theme(s) can you identify?</u>

<u>What's the most pressing issue?</u>

<u>What are the missing facts?</u>

Who is directly and indirectly involved?

What are some hypothetical situations and solutions? Frame using the *if/then* structure.

Question 6

Tell us about a relationship that you have made work despite your differences.

<u>What type of question is this?</u>

<u>What's the most pressing issue?</u>

<u>What is the best strategy?</u>

Question 7

How would you go about teaching one of your grandparents how to use a smartphone, assuming they've never used one before?

What type of question is this?

What's the most pressing issue?

What is the best strategy?

Question 8

Our program is a leader in global health. What is one such issue that you're passionate about? How do you propose we, in the medical profession, can tackle this issue?

What type of question is this?

What's the most pressing issue?

What is the best strategy?

Question 9

Tell us about a time you had to make a quick judgment call about something. What was the outcome?

<u>What type of question is this?</u>

<u>What's the most pressing issue?</u>

<u>What is the best strategy?</u>

Question 10

What do you like most about our program's curriculum and culture?

What type of question is this?

What's the most pressing issue?

What is the best strategy?

CHAPTER XIV

The Final Secret of Successful Applicants

We hope you enjoyed the book. We certainly have enjoyed teaching you what we know. As promised, we held nothing back and included everything we teach to our students in our interview prep programs found at BeMoMedInterview.com. We are confident that practicing with our strategies will take you a long way, but there is one missing piece of the puzzle we were not able to include in this book: expert feedback. In our experience, applicants improve the most when they take advantage of our realistic online mock interviews and get personal feedback from one of our experts. Of our successful students, 76% have participated in our interview preparation programs that provide this service.

Here is how our interview preparation programs work in 3 simple steps:

Step 1: We pick the best experts for you. Our consultants work remotely, so we are not limited to a small talent pool in a narrow geographical location, and we can look for the best experts anywhere in the world. We screen dozens of M.D. and Ph.D. applicants every month. The multi-step application process is rigorous and involves a functional test, an online assessment, and an online panel interview with our senior team, including our CEO, Dr. Behrouz Moemeni. Only 5% of all applicants get hired, which means we are as selective with our candidates as many medical schools. After new applicants are hired, they receive extensive training from our lead trainers, after which they continue to be monitored for 6 months before they become permanent members of our team. Our core team is thus composed of highly qualified, fully committed individuals who are there to support you through your medical school application journey.

Step 2: Join us for a mock interview session and learn our proven strategies directly from one of our experts. Our experts will not only show you how to answer interview questions, make sound judgements, manage your stress, and communicate effectively, they will tailor the feedback to your unique needs by identifying your strengths and weaknesses. We are committed to teaching you skills that last a lifetime, not cheap tricks just to get around the interview.

Step 3: Let us help you monitor your progress using a proprietary scoring system. We score students on multiple variables, including verbal communication, non-verbal communication, stress levels, ethical judgment, and so forth. This numeric scoring method gives us quantitative data so we can evaluate each student's performance objectively, rather than subjectively based on our fleeting impressions. You can continue to practice and receive feedback from our admissions experts until they are confident that you are 100% ready for your interview. Yes, that's right! Some of our programs include unlimited mock interviews with expert feedback!

Furthermore, all of our programs are backed by a 100% Satisfaction Guarantee™ and some even include our Get In Or Your Money Back® guarantee.

These are all the reasons why we are trusted by applicants who do not want to leave their success up to chance. If you are serious about acing your interview and getting into your dream program, go to BeMoMedInterview.com to learn more now. We look forward to working with you!

CHAPTER XV

Bonus Resources and Free Sample Simulated Mock Interview

Here are additional resources to help you prepare for your interviews.

Free online mock med interview simulator via access to BeMo's revolutionary InterviewProf™ platform:

SampleMedInterview.com

BeMo's private MMI test prep MasterMind Facebook Group:

https://www.facebook.com/groups/BeMo.MMIPrep.MasterMind/

BeMo's Ultimate Pre-Med Resource Center:

https://bemoacademicconsulting.com/premed-resources

Medical School Interview Preparation: Is it Important to Seek Professional Help?:

https://bemoacademicconsulting.com/blog/medical-school-interview-preparation

How To Prepare For Your Med School Interview:

https://bemoacademicconsulting.com/blog/how-to-prepare-for-med-school-interview

How To Ace Your Panel, Traditional or Conversational Med School Interview:

https://bemoacademicconsulting.com/blog/how-to-ace-panel-traditional-conversational-med-school-interview

Medical School Interview Questions: 110 Common Questions With Expert Advice!:

https://bemoacademicconsulting.com/blog/common-med-school-interview-questions

"When Do You Hear Back from Medical Schools for Interviews?":

https://bemoacademicconsulting.com/blog/when-do-you-hear-back-from-medical-schools-for-interviews

BeMo's 200 sample MMI questions:

https://bemoacademicconsulting.com/blog/sample-mmi-practice-questions

BeMo's MMI prep blog:

https://bemoacademicconsulting.com/blog/category-multiple-mini-interview.html

Made in the USA
Columbia, SC
01 December 2020

26018468R00173